FUNDAMENTAL OF SOFTWARE ENGINEERING

PROF. RAHENAAZ PATHAN

Made with ♥ on the Notion Press Platform
www.notionpress.com

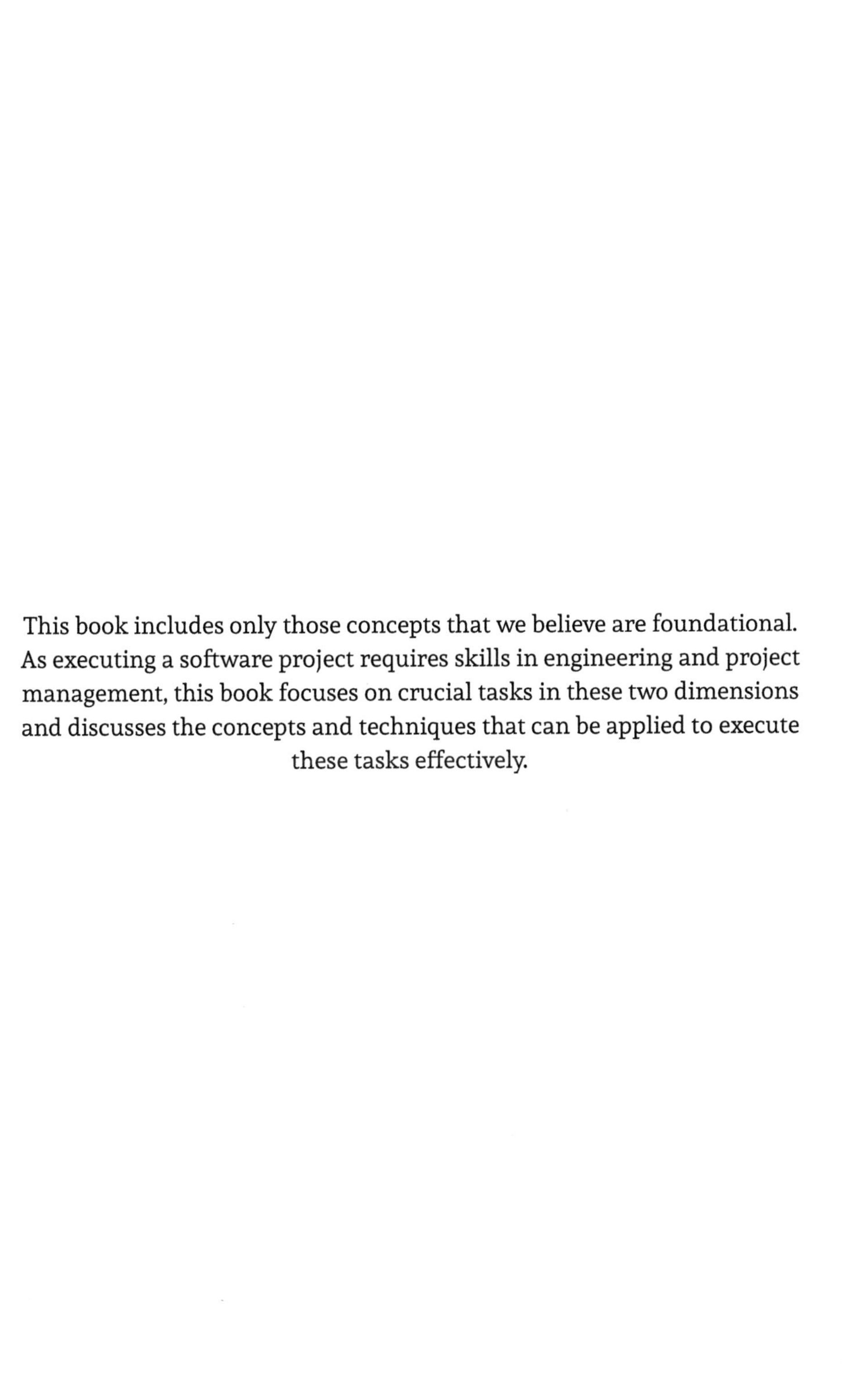

This book includes only those concepts that we believe are foundational. As executing a software project requires skills in engineering and project management, this book focuses on crucial tasks in these two dimensions and discusses the concepts and techniques that can be applied to execute these tasks effectively.

Contents

FOREWORD

If you want to learn any trend and technologies and you are willing to create any software application and work on any project so you need to clear your basic concepts of that particular domain. Software engineering is basically useful to create connection between many devices and connected applications. You can gain the concepts with different project management ideas how to build project and manage it.

PREFACE

This book is for computer scientists,computer engineers and others who wants to learn about basic with software development and project management.

Our aim is to explain the enduring concepts underlying all computer system, and to show you the concrete ways that these ideas affect the correctness, performance, and utility of your project development and management.

If you study and learn the concepts in this book, you will be on your way to becoming the rare "power developer" who knows how things work and how to fix them. Our aim is to present the fundamental concepts in ways that you will find useful right away. You will also be prepared to studying such topics as anlaysis of software, software project management, software testing.

Acknowledgements

I would like to express my greatest appreciation to the all individuals who have helped and supported me throughout writing this book. I am thankful to my family members and my colleagues during this book writing for initial advice, and encouragement, which led to the final completion of the book.

I special acknowledgment goes to my motivators who helped me in completing the book by exchanging interesting ideas and sharing their experience. Also i like to thanks to Parul University from where i got the uncountable and a lot of knowledge.

I would like to thank my special one Mr. Faizan Shaikh who always motivated me to do my best in my career also Thank you for always believing in me.

I wish to thank my parents as well for their undivided support and interest who inspired me and encouraged me to go my own way, without whom I would be unable to complete this book.

In the end, I want to thank my friends who displayed appreciation for my work and motivated me to continue my work.

Prologue

In this book the basic details of basic with analysis of software, software project management, software testing as well as how to construct a model and software myth, and requirement of the software.

before creating and software learning basic concepts of models activity diagram, data flow diagram and basic function and equation about models.

Using Software management and analysis we can manage our project and develop the best project.

I

Software Development Process

Software

Software "is more than just a program code. A program is an executable code, which serves some computational purpose. Software is considered to be collection of executable programming code, associated libraries and documentations. Software, when made for a specific requirement is called **software" product.**

Software"are of two"types.

- System"Software"
- Application"Software"

System "Software:"It"is responsible for controlling, integrating the hardware components of a system so"the software"and the users can work with"them.

Example:"Operating"System.

Application Software:"It is used to accomplish some specific task."It should be collection of small"programs.

Example: Microsoft Word, Excel etc.

SOFTWARE "CHARACTERISTICS"

The "characteristics of software decide whether the software is good or bad.'

Understandability:

- Software"should be easy to understand"
- It"should be efficient to use"

Cost:

- Software"should be cost effective as per its usage"

Maintainability:

- Software"should be easily maintainable and modifiable in future"

Modularity:

- Software "should have modular approach so it can be handled effortlessly for" testing.

Functionality

- Software should be practically proficient to meet client necessities.

Reliability

- It "should have the ability to provide failure free" service.

Portability

- Software should have the capability to be adapted for different environments.

Correctness

- Software "should be correct as per its " requirements.

Documentation

- Software should be appropriately recorded with the goal that we can re-allude it in future.

Reusability

- It should be reusable, or its code or logic should be reusable in future.

Interoperability

- Software "should be able to communicate with various devices using standard bus structure and "protocol.

Software "is engineered, not manufactured like hardware"

Software "development is same as hardware manufacturing but it is fundamentally different activity. In hardware manufacturing it introduces quality problem but it can easily correct in software development".

Once "a product is manufactured it is not possible or not easy to correct it, change it, enhance it, remove error from it without temper product or it is costly. But software can easily".

So, "the approach of construction of product is different. In case of hardware product numbers of copies generate a cost due to raw material and other manufacturing processing expenses but in case of software it is not the issue. You can create number of copies of software.

Software does not wear out"

First, we understand the characteristic of hardware. Hardware can damage after running time. As time passes hardware component suffer from effects of dust, vibration, misuse, "temperature and many other environmental effects. So, the failure rate "rises. This is the wear out of hardware.

The "bathtub curve" shown in Figure 1 depicts failure rate of hardware as a function of time. Hardware suffers high failure rate early in its life. There are three phases in hardware life.

· In "first phase failure rate is much more. But after testing and fixing bugs failure rate will come down and may stabilize after certain "time. Second "phase is useful life phase of hardware component where failure rate is approximately low and “constant. And “after few years it comes in last stage where failure rate is high and product will wear “out.

· But “software is not highly affected by environmental effects which cause hardware to wear out. The failure rate graph for software “component is "Idealized curve" shown in Figure 2.

· Undiscovered “errors will cause high failure rates early in the life of a “program. However, these “are corrected and the curve becomes flat as “shown. The "actual curve" is shown in Figure 2.

· During its “life, software will undergo change or “maintenance. As “changes are made, some new defects will be introduced, causing the failure rate curve to “spike.

· When “hardware component wears out, it is just replaced by spare “parts. There is no spare part to replace in software component. It “requires further changes in existing product or component. So, it is more complex than “hardware.

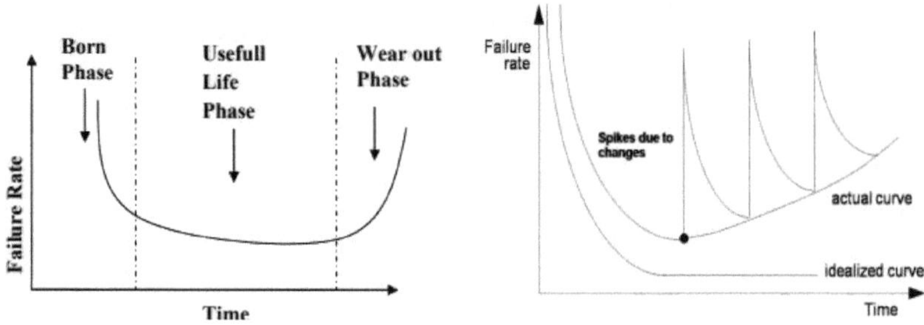

Software gives component-based construction, it gives reusability of components

· Now “a day’s industry is moving towards component-based” construction. “Efforts have been made to design standard components that may be used in new project. Software reusability has introduced another area which is known as component-based software “engineering.

· A software component should be designed and implemented so that it can be reused in many different programs.

· Once different “components are created and tested separately, at “final product each component separately not needed to “be checked or tested.

Integration of components and final product should be “tested. Graphical User Interfaces are “built using reusable components that enables the creation “of graphics window and animated menus.

Software is flexible for custom built

· A “program can be developed to do “anything.” Sometimes, this characteristic may be the best and may help us to accommodate any kind of “change. However, “most of the times, this "almost anything" characteristic has made software development difficult to plan, monitor and “control. “This unpredictability is the beginning of software “crisis.

Software Development Myths

Pressman describes managers' beliefs in the following mythology as grasping at straws:

- Development problems can be solved by developing and documenting standards. Standards have been developed by companies and standards organizations. They can be very useful. However, they are frequently ignored by developers because they are irrelevant and incomplete, and sometimes incomprehensible.
- Development problems can be solved by using state-of-the art tools. Tools may help, but there is no magic. Problem solving requires more than tools, it requires great understanding. As Fred Brooks (1987) says, there is no silver bullet to slay the software development werewolf.
- When schedules slip, just add more people This solution seems intuitive: if there is too much work for the current team, just enlarge it. Unfortunately, increasing team size increases communication overhead. New workers must learn project details taking up the time of those who are already immersed in the project. Also, a larger team has many more communication links, which slows progress. Fred Brooks (1975) gives us one of the most famous software engineering maxims, **which is not a myth**, ``adding people to a late project makes it later.‘

Software Customer Myths.

Change is easily accommodated, since software is malleable.
Software can certainly be changed, but often changes after release can

require an enormous amount of labour.

- A general statement of need is sufficient to start coding

This myth reminds me of a cartoon that I used to post on my door. It showed the software manager talking to a group of programmers, with the quote: ``You programmers just start coding while I go down and find out what they want the program to do." This scenario is an exaggeration. However, for developers to have a chance to satisfy the customers' requirements, they need detailed descriptions of these requirements. Developers cannot read the minds of customers.

- **Developer Myths**.

- The job is done when the code is delivered.
    - Commercially successful software may be used for decades. Developers must continually maintain such software: they add features and repair bugs. Maintenance costs predominate over all other costs; maintenance may be 70% of the development costs. This myth is true only for shelf ware --- software that is never used, and there are no customers for next release of a shelf ware product.

- Project success depends solely on the quality of the delivered **program**.
    - Documentation and software configuration information is very important to the quality. After functionality, maintainability, see the preceding myth, is of critical importance. Developers must maintain the software and they need good design documents, test data, etc to do their job.

- You can't assess software quality until the program is running.
    - There are static ways to evaluate quality without running a program. Software reviews can effectively determine the quality of requirements documents, design documents, test plans, and code. Formal (mathematical) analyses are often used to verify safety critical software, software security factors, and very-high reliability software.

- **SOFTWARE ENGINEERING**
- Software engineering is the application of principles used in the field of engineering, which usually deals with physical systems, to the design, development, testing, deployment and management of software systems.
- Software engineering is the process of analyzing user needs and designing, constructing, and testing end user applications that will satisfy these needs through the use of software programming languages.
- A software engineer is a person who applies the principles of software engineering to the design, development, maintenance, testing, and evaluation of computer software.
- "Software engineering is the application of a symmetric, disciplined and quantifiable approach to the development, operation and maintenance of software."
- Software engineering tells how s/w will work with machines.
- Software engineering covers technical and management issues.
- **SOFTWARE ENGINEERING LAYERED APPROACH**

- Software engineering can be viewed as a layered technology. Actually, software engineering is totally a layered technology.
- It encompasses process, methods, tools that enables a s/w product to be built in a timely manner.

- Four layers are there.
- Quality
- Process
- Method
- Tools

1. A quality Process: -

- SE mainly focuses on quality product.
- It checks whether the output meets with its requirement specifications or not.
- Every organization should maintain its total quality management.
- This layer supports software engineering.

2. **Process: -**

- It is the heart of the SE.
- It is a foundation layer for development.
- s/w process is a set of activities together if ordered and performed properly, the desired result would be produced.
- Define framework activities.

3. Methods: -

- SE methods provide the "Technical Questions" for building Software. Methods contain a broad array of tasks that include communication requirement analysis, design modeling, program construction testing and support.
- It describes 'how-to' build software product.
- It creates SE environment to software product using CASE tools.

4. Tools: -

- SE tools provide automated or semi-automated support for the "Process" and the "Methods". Tools are combined and interrelated so that information created by one tool can be used by another.

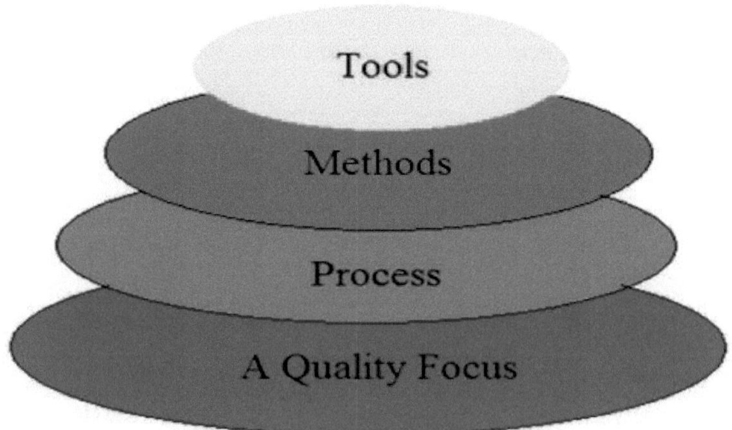

NEED OF SOFTWARE ENGINEERING?

- To help developers to obtain high quality software product.
- To develop the product in appropriate manner using life cycle models.
- To acquire skills to develop large programs.
- To acquire skills to be a better programmer.
- To provide a software product in a timely manner.
- To provide a quality software product.
- To provide a software product at a agreed cost.
- To develop ability to solve complex programming problems.
- Also learn techniques of: specification, design, user interface development, testing, project management, etc.

SOFTWARE DEVELOPMENT

- Software development is the process of developing software through successive phases in an orderly way.
- This process includes not only the actual writing of code but also the preparation of requirements and objectives, the design of what is to be coded, and confirmation that what is developed has met objectives.

Three most common being for software development.

- To meet specific needs of specific clients.
- To meet a perceived need of some set of potential users.
- To develop for personal use.
- Software development process is a set of steps that a software program goes through when developed.
- General phases of software development are:

    - Requirements
    - Design
    - Implementation
    - Testing
    - Verification
    - Documentation

- Maintenance.

IMPORTANCE OF SOFTWARE DEVELOPMENT

- Software is important to **make the *hardware working.***
- Software is important to ***build up security*** where it needs to be done, such as, in banks, money transaction etc.
- Software is important to ***make a task easier***, such as, distribution of products, products information etc.
- Software is important to use the computers power or working efficiency to perform those tasks which cannot be done or controlled by human.
- it can be said that software is important to make things easier, faster, more reliable and safer.

GENERIC FRAMEWORK ACTIVITIES AND UMBRELLAACTIVITIES:

- **Software Process:**
  - Process defines a framework for a set of Key Process Areas (KPAs) that must be established for effective delivery of software engineering technology.
  - This establishes the context in which technical methods are applied, work products such as models, documents, data, reports, forms, etc. are produced, milestones are established, quality is ensured, and change is properly managed.

- In other words, Software development is the computer programming, documenting, testing and bug fixing involved in creating and maintaining application and frameworks involved in a software release life cycle and resulting in a software product.

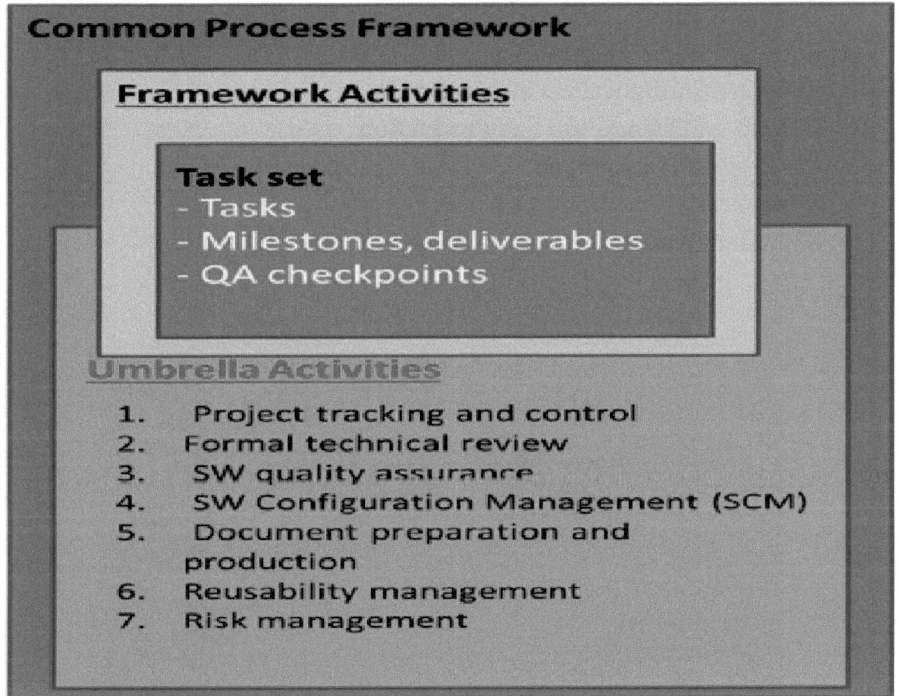

These above described five activities can be used in any kind of software development: -

- **<u>Communication:</u>** This activity involves heavy communication with customers and other stakeholders in order to gather requirements and other related activities.
- **<u>Planning:</u>** Here a plan to be followed will be created which will describe the technical tasks to be conducted, risks, required resources, work schedule etc.
- **<u>Modelling:</u>** A model will be created to better understand the requirements and design to achieve these requirements.
- **<u>Construction:</u>** Here the code will be generated and tested.
- **<u>Deployment:</u>** Here, a complete or partially complete version of the software is represented to the customers to evaluate and they give feedbacks based on the evaluation.

- Software Project Tracking and Control
- Formal Technical Review
- Software Quality Assurance
- Software Configuration Management
- Document Preparation and Production
- Reusability Management
- Measurement
- Risk Management

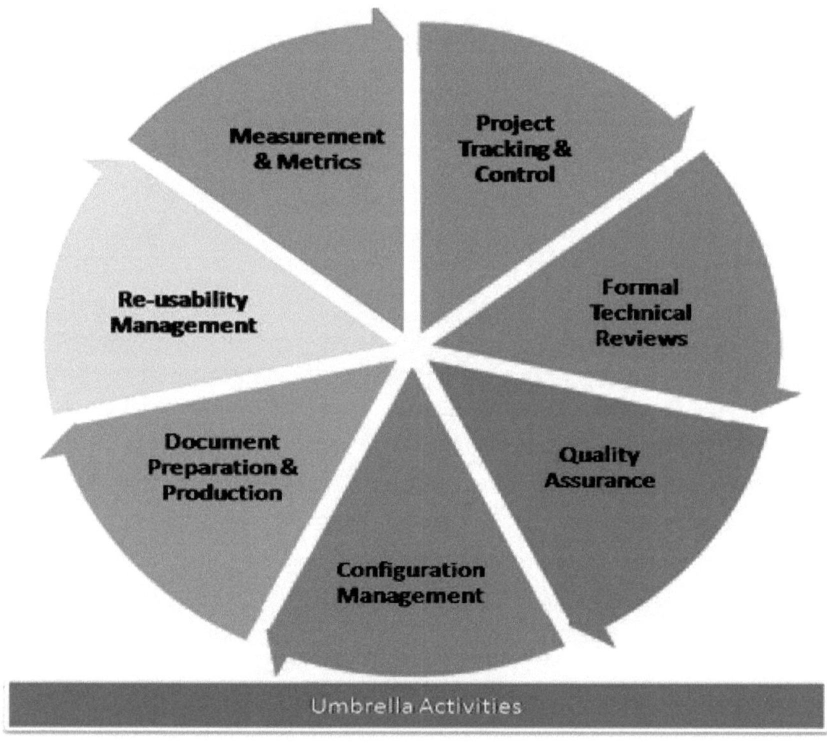

1. Software Project Tracking and Control

- When plan, tasks, models all have been done then a network of software engineering tasks that will enable to get the job done on time will have to be created.

2. Formal Technical Review

- This includes reviewing the techniques that has been used in the project.

3. Software Quality Assurance

- This is very important to ensure the quality measurement of each part to ensure them.

4. Software Configuration Management

- Software configuration management (SCM) is a set of activities designed to control change by identifying the work products that are likely to change, establishing relationships among them, defining mechanisms for managing different versions of these work products.

5. Document Preparation and Production

- All the project planning and other activities should be hardly copied and the production get started here.

6. Reusability Management

- This includes the backing up of each part of the software project they can be corrected or any kind of support can be given to them later to update or upgrade the software at user/time demand.

7. Measurement

- This will include all the measurement of every aspects of the software project.

8. Risk Management

Risk management is a series of steps that help a software team to understand and manage uncertainty. It's a really good idea to identify it, assess its probability of occurrence, estimate its impact, and establish a contingency plan that— 'should the problem actually occur'.

SOFTWARE DEVELOPMENT MODELS / LIFE CYCLE MODELS

- Every system has a life cycle. It begins when a problem is recognized, after then system is developed, grows until maturity and then maintenance needed due to change in the nature of the system.
- SDLC is defined as "structured sequence of phases to implement an information system (Software)".
- The ultimate goal of system analysis and design is to produce good quality maintainable software within reasonable time frame and at low cost.
- If you want to produce such successful system then the system has to pass through some procedures which are known as phases.
- A software life cycle model is also called a Software Development Life Cycle (SDLC).
- Software life cycle model (process model)à is a descriptive and diagrammatic representation of the software life cycle.
- A life cycle model represents all the activities required to make a software product transit through its life cycle phases.
- General stages à feasibility study, requirement analysis and specification, design, coding, testing and maintenance.
- Every software development process model includes system requirements as input and deliverable product as output.

NEED OF LIFE CYCLE MODELS

- Provide generic guidelines for developing a suitable process for a project.
- It provides improvement and guarantee of quality product.
- Without using of a particular life cycle model, the development of a software product would not be in a systematic and disciplined manner.
- Provide monitoring the progress.
- Defines entry and exit criteria.
- The documentation of life cycle models enhances the understanding between developers and client.

SOFTWARE LIFE CYCLE MODELS

- Waterfall Model
- Incremental Model
- RAD Model
- Prototyping Model
- Spiral Model

WATERFALL MODEL

- The Waterfall Model is the first Process Model to be introduced. It is very simple to understand and use.
- In a Waterfall model, each phase must be completed before the next phase can begin and there is no overlapping in the phases.
- Waterfall model is the pioneer of the SDLC processes.
- In "The Waterfall" approach, the whole process of software development is divided into separate phases.
- The outcome of one phase acts as the input for the next phase sequentially.
- This means that any phase in the development process begins only if the previous phase is complete.
- Different phases are as follows:

    - Requirement Analysis
    - System Design
    - Implementation
    - System Testing
    - System Deployment
    - System maintenance

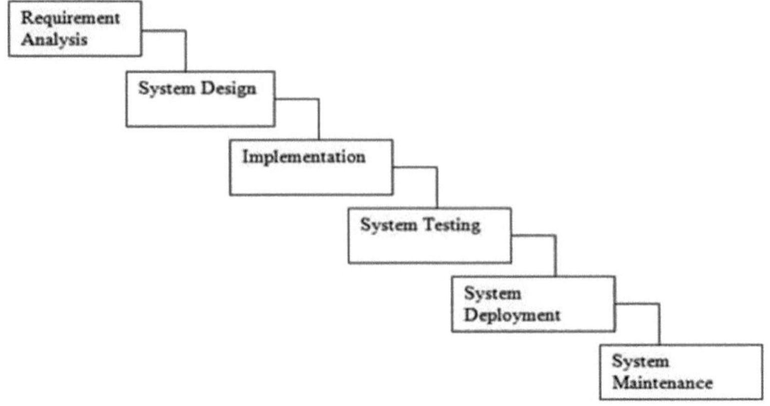

1. Requirement Analysis

- In this phase, capture all the requirements of customer.
- The first phase involves understanding what need to be design and what is its function, purpose etc.
- Here, the specifications of the input and output or the final product are studied and marked in this phase.

2. System Design

- As per the requirements, create the design
- Capture the hardware / software requirements.
- Document the designs

3. Implementation

- After, system design project manager creates the programs / code.
- Integrate the codes for the next phase.
- After implementation manager do the unit testing of the code.
- With inputs from system design, the system is first developed in small programs called units, which are integrated in the next phase. Each unit is developed and tested for its functionality which is referred to as Unit Testing.

4. System Testing

- All the units developed in the implementation phase are integrated into a system after testing of each unit. The software designed, needs to go through constant software testing to find out if there are any flaw or errors. Testing is done so that the client does not face any problem during the installation of the software.

5. System Deployment

- Once the functional and non-functional testing is done, the product is deployed in the customer environment or released into the market.

6. System maintenance

- This step occurs after installation, and involves making modifications to the system or an individual component to alter attributes or improve performance. These modifications arise either due to change requests initiated by the customer, or defects uncovered during live use of the system. Client is provided with regular maintenance and support for the developed software.

WHEN TO USE SDLC WATERFALL MODEL?

- Requirements are stable and not changed frequently.
- An application is small.
- There is no requirement which is not understood or not very clear.
- The environment is stable.
- The tools and technology used is stable and is not dynamic.
- Resources are well trained and are available.

ADVANTAGES

- Simple and easy to understand and use.
- For smaller projects, waterfall model works well and yield the appropriate results.
- Since the phases are rigid and precise, one phase is done one at a time, it is easy to maintain.

- The entry and exit criteria are well defined, so it easy and systematic to proceed with quality.
- Results are well documented.

DISADVANTAGES

- Cannot adopt the changes in requirements
- It becomes very difficult to move back to the phase. For example, if the application has now moved to the testing stage and there is a change in requirement, It becomes difficult to go back and change it.
- Delivery of the final product is late as there is no prototype which is demonstrated intermediately.
- Not suitable for the projects where requirements are changed frequently.

INCREMENTAL MODEL

- The incremental build model is a method of software development where the model is designed, implemented and tested incrementally (a little more is added each time) until the product is finished.
- It involves both development and maintenance. The product is defined as finished when it satisfies all of its requirements.
- Incremental Model is a process of software development where requirements are broken down into multiple standalone modules of software development cycle.
- Incremental development is done in steps from analysis design, implementation, testing/verification, maintenance.
- we can analyses that at the initial stage, core module/product is developed. Then by adding customer requirements or new functionalities the incremental version is built.

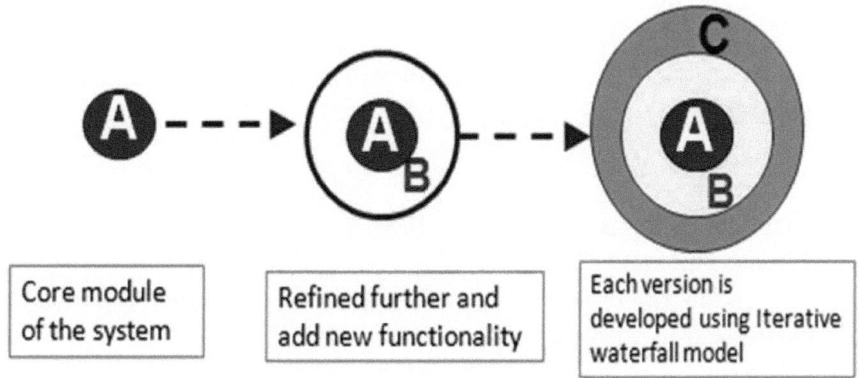

- It involves both development and maintenance. The product is defined as finished when it satisfies all of its requirements.
- It is also referred as the successive version of waterfall model using incremental approach and evolutionary model.
- In this model, the system is broken down into several modules which can be incrementally implemented and delivered.
- First develop the core product of the system. The core product is used by customers to evaluate the system.
- The initial product skeleton is refined into increasing levels of capability: by adding new functionalities in successive versions.

ADVANTAGES

- The software will be generated quickly during the software life cycle
- It is flexible and less expensive to change requirements and scope
- Thought the development stages changes can be done
- This model is less costly compared to others
- A customer can respond to each building
- Errors are easy to be identified

DISADVANTAGES

- Sometimes it is difficult to subdivide problems into functional units.

- Model can be used for very large problems.
- planning and design.

RAD MODEL

- RAD model is Rapid Application Development model. It is a type of incremental model.
- In RAD model the components or functions are developed in parallel as if they were mini projects.
- It focuses on input-output source and destination of the information. the larger projects are divided into a series of smaller projects.
- The main features of RAD model are that it focuses on the reuse of templates, tools, processes, and code.

RAD MODEL HAS THE FOLLOWING PHASES

- Business Modelling
- Data Modelling
- Process Modelling
- Application Generation
- Testing and Turnover

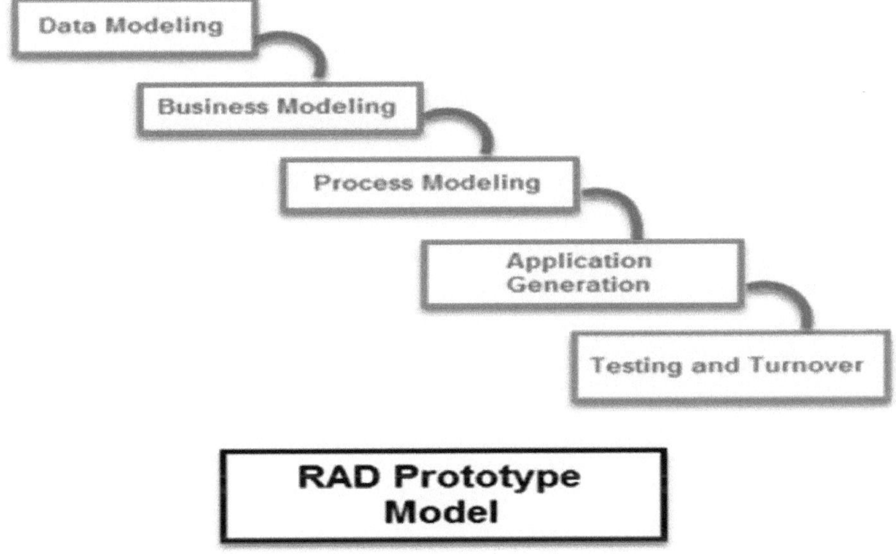

The phases in the rapid application development (RAD) model are:

1. **Business modeling:**

- The information flow is identified between various business functions.
- On basis of the flow of information and distribution between various business channels, the product is designed

1. **Data modeling:**

- Information gathered from business modeling is used to define data objects that are needed for the business.
- The information collected from business modeling is refined into a set of data objects that are significant for the business.

3. **Process modeling:**

- Data objects defined in data modeling are converted to achieve the business information flow to achieve some specific business objective.

- The data object that is declared in the data modeling phase is transformed to achieve the information flow necessary to implement a business function

4. **Application generation:**

- Automated tools are used to convert process models into code and the actual system.

5. **Testing and turnover:**

- Test new components and all the interfaces.
- As prototypes are individually tested during every iteration, the overall testing time is reduced in RAD.

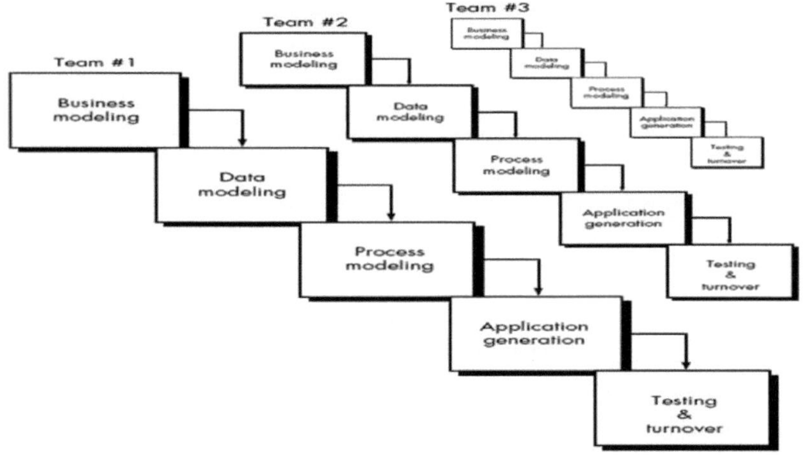

ADVANTAGES

- Application can be developed in a quick time.
- This model highly makes use of reusable components.
- Reduce time for developing and testing.
- Customer satisfaction is improved due to full involvement.

DISADVANTAGES

- Requirement must be cleared and well understood for this model.
- It is not well suited where technical risk is high.
- In it, highly skilled and expert developers are needed.

PROTOTYPE MODEL

- Prototype is a working physical system or sub system. Prototype is nothing but a toy implementation of a system.
- In this model, before starting actual development, a working prototype of the system should first be built.
- A prototype is actually a partial developed product.
- Compared to the actual software, a prototype usually have
    - limited functional capabilities
    - low reliability
    - Inefficient performance
- It is built using several shortcuts.
- It is very useful in developing GUI part of system.
- It turns out to be a very crude version of the actual system.
- In working of the prototype model, product development starts with initial requirements gathering phase.
- Then, quick design is carried out and prototype is built.
- The developed prototype is then submitted to the customer for his evaluation.
- Based on customer feedback, the requirements are refined and prototype is modified.
- This cycle of obtaining customer feedback and modifying the prototype continues till the customers approve the prototype.
- The actual system is developed using the different phases of iterative waterfall model.

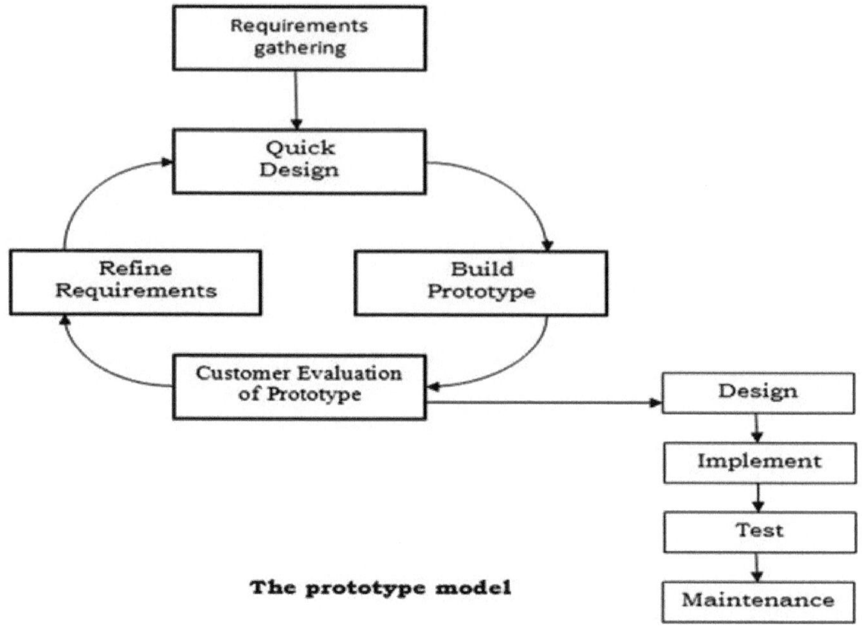

The prototype model

ADVANTAGES

- Customers can get a chance to have a look of the product.
- New requirements can be accommodated easily.
- Missing functionalities identified quickly.
- It provides better flexibility in design and development.
- More chance of user satisfaction.

DISADVANTAGES

- Wasting of time is there because core product is thrown away.
- The construction cost is very high.
- This model requires extensive participation and involvement of the customers that is not possible every time.
- If end user is not satisfied with the initial prototype, he may lose interest in the final product.

SPIRAL MODEL

- In application development, spiral model uses fourth generation (4GL) languages and developments tools.
- The diagrammatic representation of this model appears like a spiral with many loops.
- Each loop of the spiral represents a phase of the software process:
- the innermost loop might be concerned with system feasibility,
- the next loop with system requirements definition,
- the next one with system design, and so on.
- No fixed number of phases is there in this model.
- This model is more flexible compared with other models.
- Each loop in the spiral is split into four sectors (quadrants)

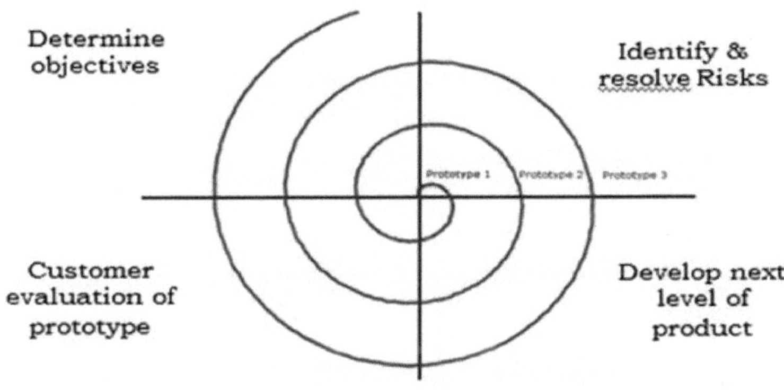

Spiral model

1st Quadrant: Determine objectives

- **Identifying the objectives, their relationships and find the possible alternative solutions.**
- **Also examine the risks associated with these objectives.**

2nd Quadrant: Identify and resolve risks

- **Detailed analysis is carried out of each identified risk.**
- **Alternate solutions are evaluated and risks are reducing at this quadrant.**

3rd Quadrant: Develop next level of product

- Develop and validate the next level of the product.
- Activities like design, code development, code inspection, testing and packaging are performed.
- Resolution of critical operations and technical issues of next level product are performed.

4th Quadrant: Customer evaluation (Review and Planning)

- In this part, review the results achieved.
- Plan the next iteration around the spiral. Different plans like development plan, test plan, installation plan is performed.

ADVANTAGES

- It is more flexible, as we can easily deal with changes.
- Due to user involvement, user satisfaction is improved.
- It provides cohesion between different stages.
- Risks are analysed and resolved so final product will be more reliable.
- New idea and additional functionalities can be easily added at later stage.

DISADVANTAGES

- It is more complex to understand.
- It is applicable for large problem only.
- It can be more costly to use.
- More number of documents are needed as a greater number of spirals.

II

Software Analysis and Design

Requirement gathering and Analysis

- **Requirement**

- A thing that is needed or wanted.
- Requirement is playing **key role** to develop
- Done by Business analyst (Market) & system analyst (Company)
- Removing all **ambiguities and inconsistencies** from customer **perception.**
- Mainly **two activities** are concerned with this task.

  1) Requirement gathering
  2) Requirement analysis
  Requirement gathering:

- It is usually **the first part** of any software product.
- **This is the base** for the whole development effort.
- **Goal** à to collect all relevant information from the customer regarding the product to be developed.
- This is **done to clearly understand the customer requirements** so that incompleteness and inconsistencies are removed.

Requirement analysis

- **Goal** à to clearly understand the exact requirement of the customer.
- **requirements analysis** as (1) the process of studying user needs to arrive at a definition of a system, hardware or software requirements. (2) The process of studying and refining system, hardware or software requirements.
- Requirements analysis helps to understand, interpret, classify, and organize the software requirements.

Software requirement specification

- SRS is the output of requirement gathering and analysis activity.
- SRS is a **detailed description** of the software that is to be developed.
- It describes the **complete behavior** the system.
- It describes **what** the proposed system should do without describing **how** the software will do.
- It is working as a **reference document** to the developer.
- It **provides guideline** for project development.

- SRS is actually **serving as a contract** between developer and end user.
- The SRS **translates the ideas** of the customers (input) into the formal documents (output).

Benefits of SRS.

- SRS provides **foundation for design** work.
- It **enhances communication** between customer and developer.
- Developers can get the idea **what exactly the customer wants.**
- It enables project planning and helps in verification and validation process.
- High quality SRS **reduces the development cost and time** efforts.

Design Process

  - The design process is a sequence of steps to describe all aspects of the software.
  - It specifies *how* aspect of the system.

- Purpose à plan a solution of the problem specified in SRS.
- It includes: user interface design, i/o design, data design, process and program design and technical specification etc.
- It converts SRS into program appropriate form for implementation.
- Output à design documents.

Classification of design activities:

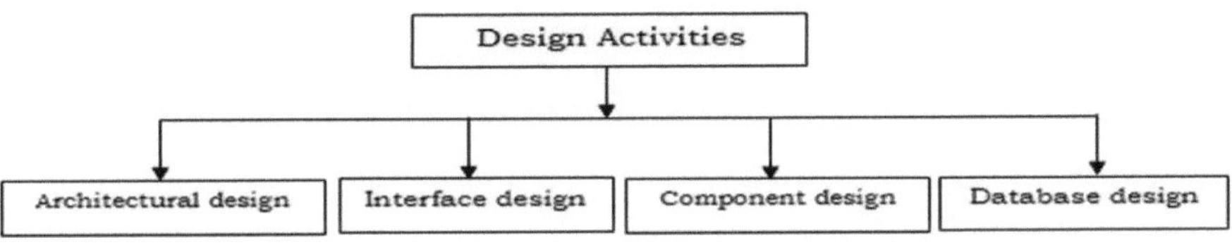

Design activities

<u>1) Architectural design:</u>

- Identify overall structure of the system, subsystem, modules and their relationship.
- Can be represented using DFD.

<u>2) Interface design</u>

- Defines the interface between system components.
- It describes how system communicates with itself and with the user also.

<u>3) Component design</u>

- Defines each system component and show how they operate.
- It can be derived from State transition diagram.

<u>4) Database design:</u>

- Defines the data structure of the system.
- Existing database can be reused or a new database to be created.

Classification of design methodologies:

- Design methodologies are followed in software development from beginning up to the completion of the product.
- Used to provide guidelines for the design activity.
- The nature of the design methodologies are dependent on the following factors:

The software development environment	Qualification and training of the development team
The type of the system being developed	Available software and hardware
User requirements	

- Classification of design methodologies is shown in the figure.

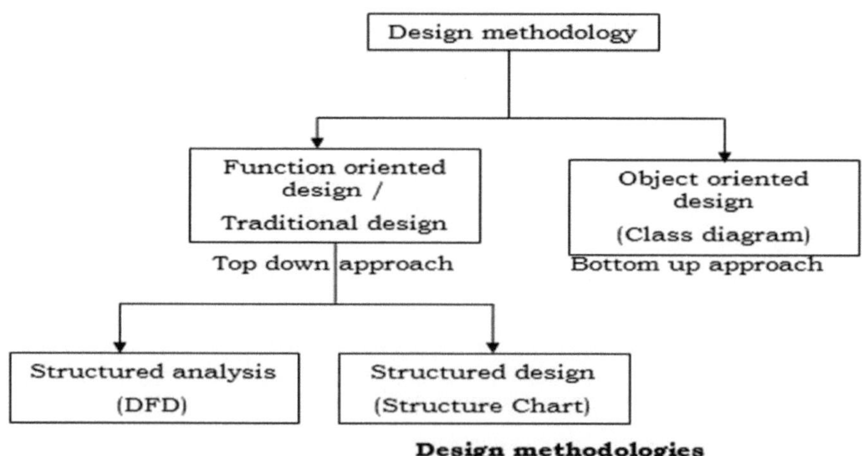

Design methodologies

1) Function oriented design

- Set of functions are described.

- Top down approach.
- Data in the system is centralized and shared among different functions.
- Function oriented design further classified into à Structure analysis and Structure design.

2) Object oriented design

- Objects and their relationships are identified.
- It is built using bottom-up approach.
- Each object is a member of class.

Cohesion and Coupling

- Modularity is a good property of software development.
- Modular system
- Cohesion and coupling are two modularization criteria.
- ***'high cohesion and low coupling'*** is needed for good development.

Cohesion

- It isa measure of functional strength of a module.
- **Cohesion keeps the internal modules together, and represents the functional strength.**
- Cohesion of a module represents how tightly bound the internal elements of a module are to one another.

Classification of cohesion.

Coincidental	Logical	Temporal	Procedural	Communicational	Sequential	Functional
Worst (Low)						Best (High)

1) Coincidental cohesion.

- It occurs when there are no meaningful relationships between the elements.

2) Logical cohesion.

- If there are some logical relationships between the elements of module.
- The elements perform functions that fall into same logical class.
- For example: the tasks of error handling, input and output of data.

3) Temporal cohesion.

- Temporal cohesion is same as logical cohesion except that the elements are also related in time and are executed together.

4) Procedural cohesion.

- When module contains elements that belong to common procedural unit.
- A module is said to have procedural cohesion, if the set of the module are all part of a procedure (algorithm) in which certain sequence of steps are carried out to achieve an objective.
- Example: algorithm for decoding a message.

5) Communicational cohesion.

- If all functions of the module refer to or update the same data structure. e.g. the set of functions defined on an array or a stack.
- These modules may perform more than one function together.

6) Sequential cohesion

- When the output of one element in a module forms the input to another, we get sequential cohesion.

6) Functional cohesion.

- Functional cohesion is the strongest cohesion.
- In it, all the elements of the module are related to perform a single task.
- All elements are achieving a single goal of a module.

Coupling

- Coupling between two modules is a measure of the degree of interdependence or interaction between two modules.
- Coupling refers to the no of connections between 'calling' and a 'called' module.

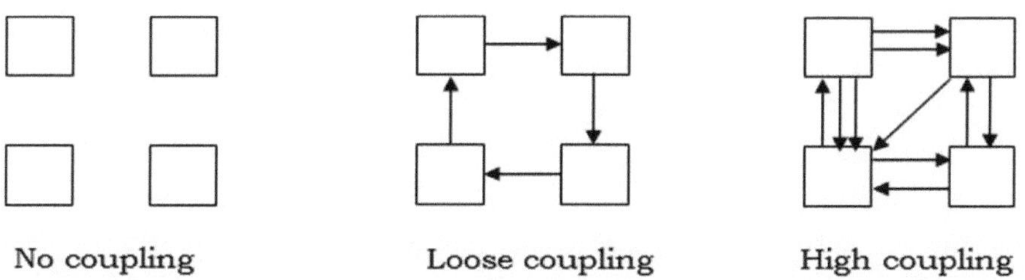

Classification of coupling

Data	Stamp	Control	Common	Content
Best (Low)				Worst (High)

1)Data coupling

- Two modules are data coupled, if they communicate using an elementary data item that is passed as a parameter between the two.
- For example: an int, a char, a float
- It is lowest coupling and best for the software development

2) Stamp coupling.

- Two modules are stamp coupled, if they communicate using a composite data item such as a record in PASCAL or a structure in C.

3) Control coupling.

- Control coupling exists between two modules, if data from one module is used to direct the order of instructions execution in another.
- Example: is a flag set in one module and tested in another module.

4) Common coupling.

- Two modules are common coupled, if they share data through some global data items.

5) Content coupling.

- Content coupling exists, if two modules share code, e.g. a branch from one module into another module.
- It is the highest coupling and creates more problems in software development.

Data Modelling Concepts

- A data model is a conceptual relationship of data structure (tables) required for a database.
- To avoid the redundancy of database, there is a need to create data model.
- Data model provides abstract and conceptual representation of data.
- Data modeling or ER diagram gives the concepts of objects, attributes and relationship between objects.

- ERD is a detailed logical representation of any system. It has three main elements à data object (entity), attributes and their relationships.

1) Data objects (Entity set)

- An entity represents a thing that has meaning and about which you want to store or record data.
- It can be external entity, a thing, an organization, a place or an event. For example: for a college à department, students, head of the department and professor may be entities.
- It has number of properties or attributes. Each object has its own attributes.

- Entities are represented using *rectangle box* and preferably written in capital letters.

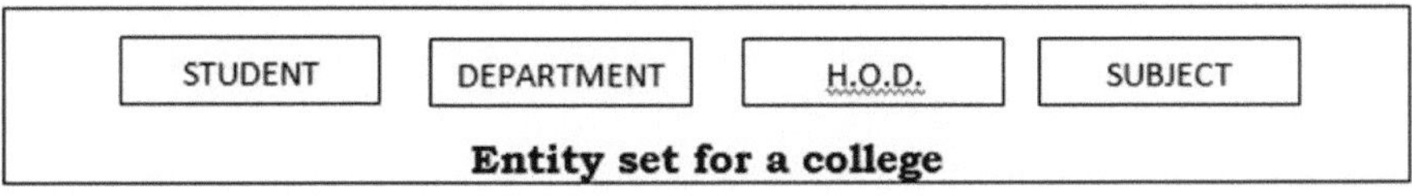

Entity set for a college

2) Attributes

- An attribute is a property or characteristic of an entity.
- Attributes provide meaning to the objects.
- Attributes must be defined as a identifier, and that become key to find instance of object.
- Attributes represented using *oval.*

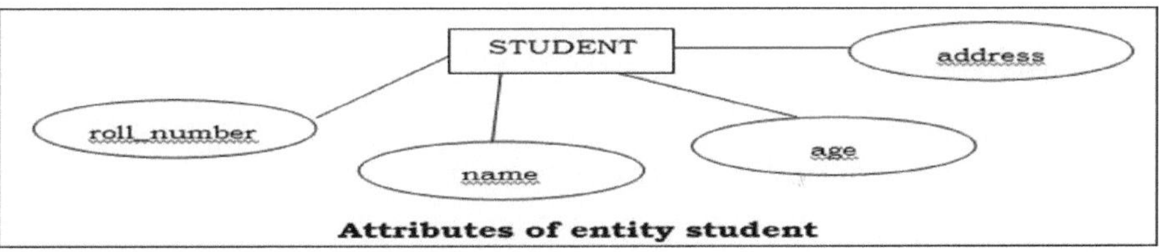

Attributes of entity student

3) Relationship

- Entities are connected to each other via relations.
- Relationship is represented using diamond shape symbol with joined relationship name.

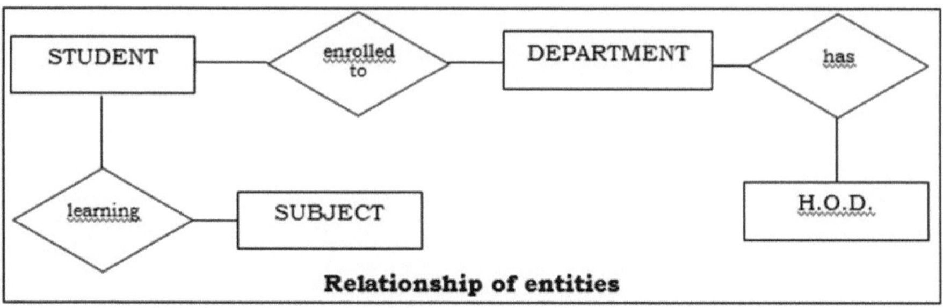

Relationship of entities

Cardinality

- The concept of cardinality defines the maximum number of objects that can participate in a relationship. That means number of occurrences of one [object] that can be related to the number of occurrences of another [object].
- Cardinality is usually expressed as simply 'one' or 'many.'
- It is also important how many occurrences of any object are related to how many occurrences of other object. This leads to a data modelling concept called cardinality.

- **Different cardinalities are explained below:**

- **One to One (1 : 1)**

  Ex à college has principal

- **One to Many (1 : M)**

  Ex à college and students

- **Many to Many (M : M)**

  Ex à students and subjects

Modality

- Modality is form of cardinality.

- Modality means a classification of relationships on the basis of whether they claim necessity, possibility or impossibility.
- The modality of relationship is 0 or optional or 1.
- The notations for modality are explained below.

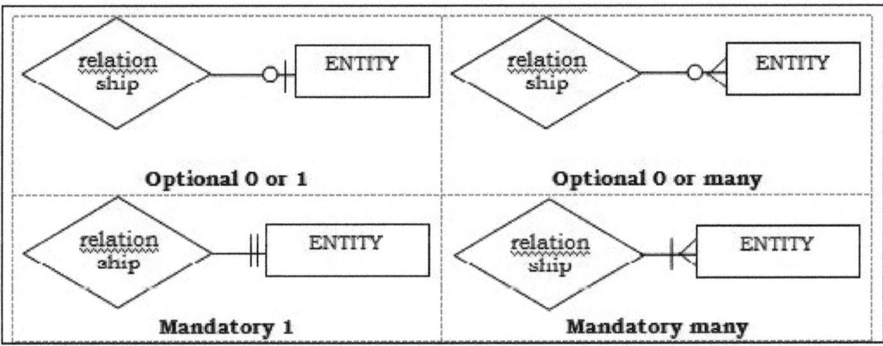

Data Flow Diagrams

- DFD (Data Flow Diagram) is also known as bubble chart or data flow graph.
- DFDs are very useful in understanding the system and can be effectively used during analysis.
- The DFD is a hierarchical graphical model of a system that shows the different processing activities or functions that the system performs and the data interchange among these functions.
- Each function is considered as a process that consumes some input data and produces some output data.

Primitive symbols used in construction of DFD model.

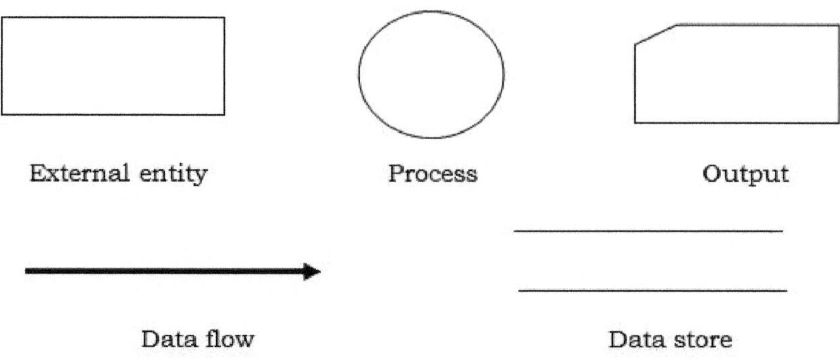

DFD symbols

1) Process:

- It is s represented by circle or bubble. Circles are annotated with names of the corresponding functions.
- A process shows the part of the system that transforms inputs into outputs.

2) External entity:

- Entity is represented by a rectangle.
- Entities are external to the system which interacts by inputting data to the system or by consuming data produced by the system.

3) Data flow:

- Data flow is represented by an arc or by an arrow.
- It used to describe the movement of the data.
- It represents the data flow occurring between two processes, or between an external entity and a process. It passes data from one part of the system to another part.

4) Data store:

- Data store is represented by two parallel lines.
- It is generally a logical file or database.
- It can be either a data structure or a physical file on the disk.

5) Output:

- Output is used when a hardcopy is produced.

Developing DFD model of the system

- DFD starts with the most abstract level of the system (lowest level) and at each higher level, more details are introduced.
- To develop higher level DFDs, processes are decomposed into their sub functions.
- The abstract representation of the problem is also called context diagram.

Context diagram (Level 0 DFD)

- The context diagram is top level diagram; it is the most abstract data flow representation of a system.
- It only contains one process node that generalizes the function of entire system with external entities. (It represents the entire system as a single bubble.)
- Data input and output are represented using incoming and outgoing arrows.

Level 1 diagram

- To develop the level 1 DFD, we have to examine the high-level functional requirements.
- It is recommended that 3 to 7 functional requirements can be directly represented as bubbles in 1st level.

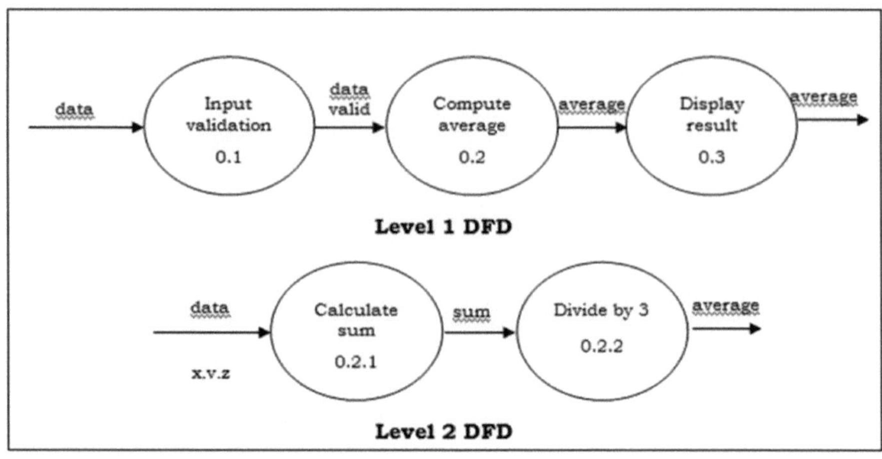

Advantages of DFD model.

- It is very simple to understand and easy to use.
- DFD can provide detailed description of the system components.
- It provides clear understanding to the developers about the system boundaries.
- It explains the logic behind the data flow within system.
- It is not only useful to represent the results of structured analysis, but also for several other applications like showing the flow of documents or items in an organization.
- Symbols used in DFD model are very less.

Disadvantages of DFD model

- Control information is not defined by a DFD.
- No specific guidance for exact decomposition,
- Sometimes it puts programmers in little confusing state.
- Different models of DFD have different symbols.

Scenario based modelling

- A scenario describes a set of actions that are performed to achieve some specific condition. And this set is specified as a sequence.

- Each step in scenario is performed by an actor or by a system.

1) UML (Unified Modeling Language)
2) Use-Case diagram
3) Activity Diagram

UML (Unified Modeling Language)

- UML is a modeling language.
- UML designs provide a standard way to visualize the design of the system.
- UML is very useful in documenting the design and analysis results.
- UML is not a design methodology.
- UML making system easy to understand using less number of primitive symbols.
- UML can be used to construct nine different types of diagrams to capture five different views of a system.
- UML diagrams provide different perspectives of the software system.

Use-Case diagram

- It provides system behavior.
- Use case model of the system consists of a set of use cases.
- Use cases represent the different ways in which a system can be used by the users.
- The purpose of a use case is to define the logical behavior of the system without knowing the internal structure of it.
- It provides understanding of the system.
- It identifies the functional requirements of the system.
- UML describes "*who can do what in a system*".
- A use case typically represents a sequence of interactions between the user and the system.

Components of use case diagram (Representation of use case diagram).

- Two main components along with relationships are used in use case diagram.

1. **Use case:**

- Represented by an ellipse with the name of the use case written inside the ellipse, named by a verb.
- All the use cases are enclosed with a rectangle representing system boundary. Rectangle contains the name of the system.
- It identifies and analyzes the fun req^n of the system.

1. **Actor:**

- An actor is anything outside the system that interacts with it, named by noun.
- Actors are represented by using the stick person icon.

3. **Relationship:**

- It is also called communication relationship. Actors are connected to use cases through relationship lines.
- An actor may have relationship with more than one use case and one-use case may relate to more than one actor.
- An actor may be a person, machine or any external system.
- Actors are connected to use cases by drawing a simple line connected to it. Actor triggers use cases.

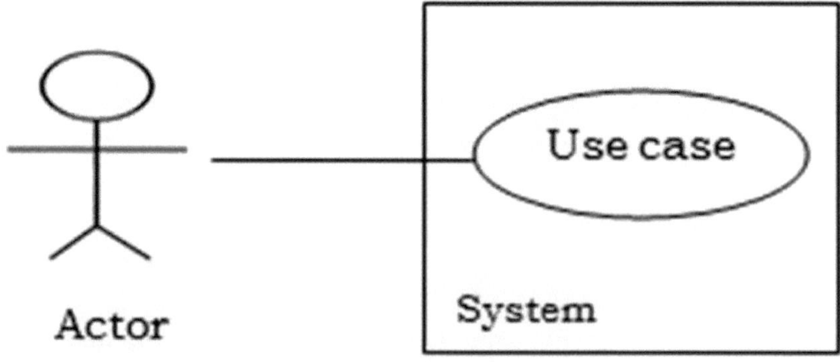

- Different relationships in use case diagram are explained below:

Association:

- It is the interface between an actor and a use case.
- It is represented by joining a line from actor to use case.

Include relationship:

- It involves one use case including the behavior of another use case.
- The "include" relationship occurs when a chunk of behavior that is similar across a number of use cases.
- It is represented using predefined stereotype <<include>>.
- Ex.

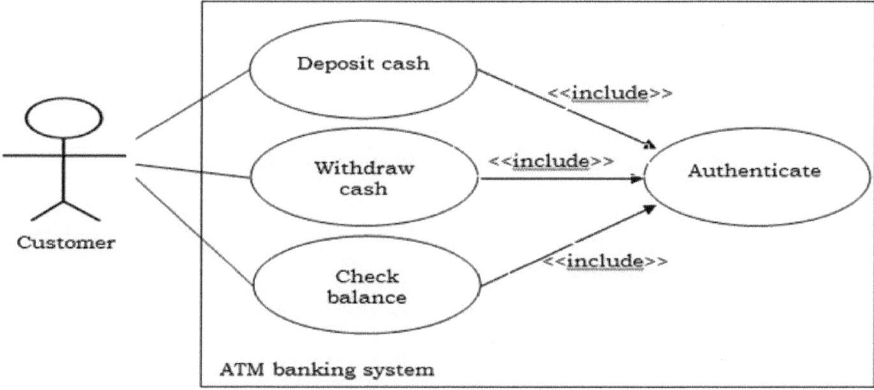

Extend relationship

- It shows optional behavior of the system.
- represented as a stereotype <<extend>>.
- Extend relationship exists when one use case calls another use case under certain condition (like: If – then condition).

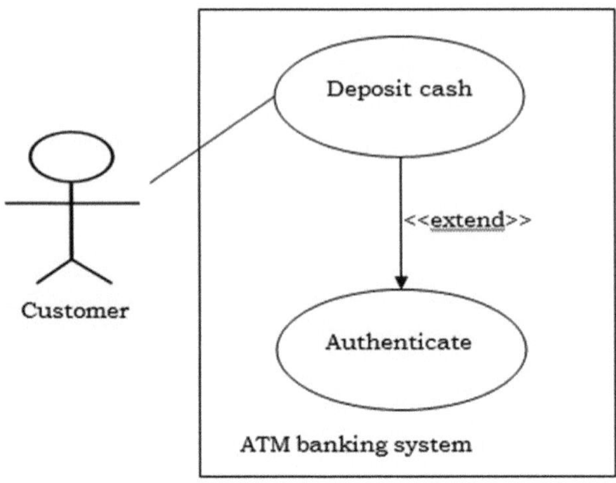

Generalization

- Used when you have one use case that is similar to another, but does slightly different.
- It is a link between use cases. In which the child use case inherits the behavior of parent use case.
- The child may override the behavior of its parent.

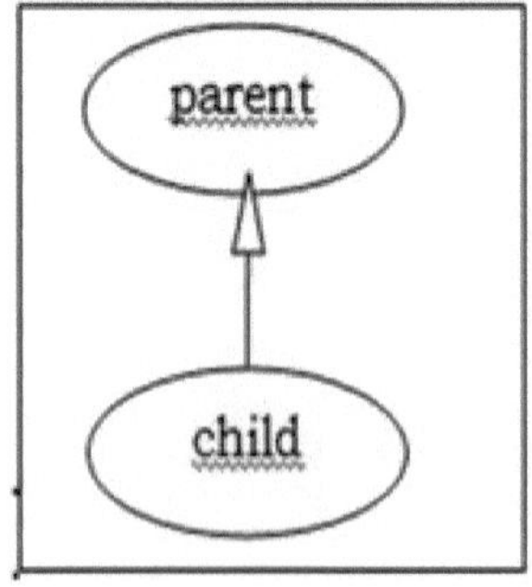

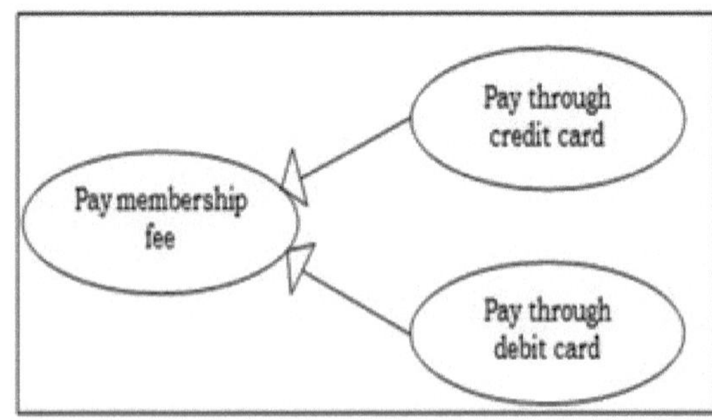

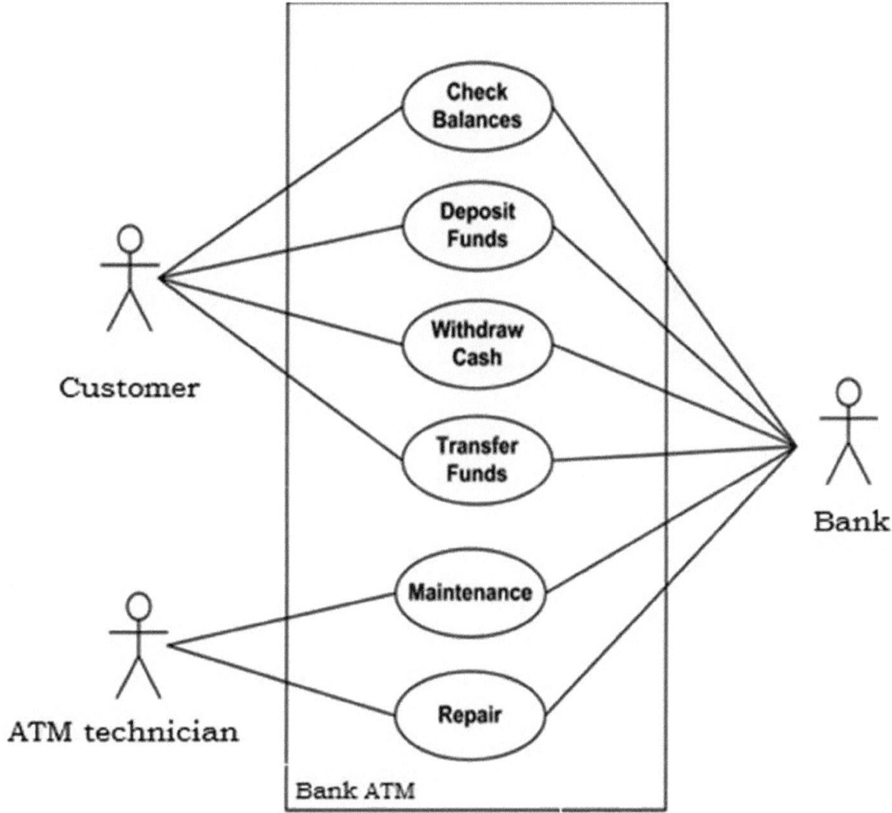

Activity Diagram

- Activity Diagrams consist of activities, states and transitions between activities and states.
- It describes how the events in a single use case relate to one another.
- It focuses on the how of activities involved in a single process.
- Activity diagrams represent workflows in a graphical way.
- Aim à to record the flow of control from one activity to another of each actor and to show interaction between them.
- It supports parallel activities.
- An activity is a state with an internal action and one or more outgoing transitions.

➞ A simple example activity diagram (ATM system).

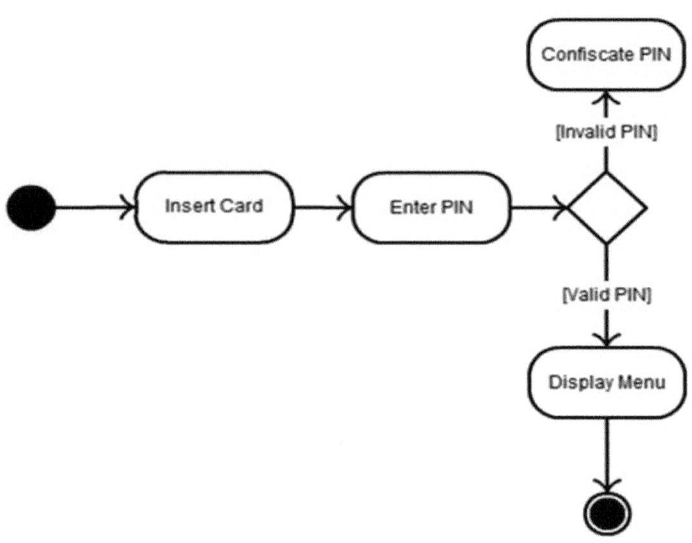

Advantages of activity diagram

- Very useful to understand complex processing activities.
- Provides understating workflow of system.
- It is good for describing synchronization and concurrency between activities.
- Provides responsibilities for interactions and associations between objects and actors.

Disadvantages of activity diagram

- Doesn't provide message part.
- It can't describe how objects collaborate.
- Complex logic can't be represented.

Difference between flowchart and activity diagram.

Flow chart	Activity diagram
- It is limited for sequential access.	- It is used for parallel and concurrent processing.
- It is used for flow of control through an algorithm, not used for object oriented procedure.	- It is usually used for object oriented systems.
- Concept of swimlanes is not there in it.	- It has the functionality of swimlanes.
- It has limited functionalities compare to activity diagram.	- It has more functionalities.

Architectural design decisions

1. Architectural views.
2. Architectural patterns.
3. Application Architecture

Software Architecture

- It is a framework that describes its form and structure, its components and how they interact together.
- To understand any complex system, we need to have the knowledge of its subsystems and their interactions.
- ***Software architecture*** is a description of the subsystems and components of a software system and the relationships between them.
- Software architecture should be of individual programs or it should be included of different sub-systems.

Architectural design

- Software architectural design is a description of how a system is organized.
- You can identify the overall structure of the system, sub-systems, modules and their relationships.
- It is derived from the DFD of the system.
- The output of architectural design is à architectural model.

Architectural design decisions

- Made by system architects.
- Based on type of system.
- Depend on functional and non-functional requirements.

Architectural views

- Architectural views represent the system as composed of types of elements and relationships between them.
- Different views expose different properties and attributes.
- Different views reduce the complexities of the system and help in understanding and analyzing the system.
- Different types of proposed architectural views are:

Module view:

- The system is viewed as a collection of code units.
- The main element in this view is modules.
- This view is code based and do not explicitly represent any runtime structure of the system.
- Examples of modules are packages, class, a method, collection of functions etc.

Conceptual view:

- It is an abstract view of the system.
- It shows detailed decompositions of the system.

Logical view:

- It shows key concepts of the system as objects and classes.
- Objects and their relationships can be identified.

Component and connector view.

- In it, system is viewed as a collection of runtime entities called components, which support in executing the system.
- While executing, components need to interact with others to support the system. And connectors provide mean for this interaction.
- Examples of connectors are pipes and sockets. Shared data can also act as connectors.

Allocation view:

- It focuses on how different software units are allocated to recourses like hardware, file systems and people.
- Allocation view specifies the relationship between software elements and environmental elements in which the software system is executed.

Process view:

- In it, system is composed of interacting process at run time.

Development view:

- It shows the breakdown structure of software into modules.

Physical view:

- It shows the system hardware and how software components are distributed across them.

Architectural patterns

- Patterns are a means of representing, sharing and reusing knowledge.
- Architectural patterns are a means of reusing knowledge about generic system architectures.

- An architectural pattern is a general, reusable solution to a commonly occurring problem in software architecture.
- It is the description of system organization.
- It provides system, subsystems and their relationships.
- Architectural patterns are often documented as software design patterns.

Commonly used architectural patterns are:

1. - Layered architecture
2. - Client-Server architecture
3. - Repository architecture (Shared data)
4. - Pipe and filter architecture

Layered architecture:

- This type of pattern describes separation and independence.
- This architecture uses many layers for allocating the different responsibilities of a software product.
- Each layer works independently and each layer can use the services offered by the layer under it.
- A well-suited example for layered architecture is OSI Layer.

Advantages:

- Increases flexibility, maintainability, and scalability.
- Changes in one layer do not affect another.
- Authentication can be provided in each layer.
- Helps you to test the components independently of each other.

Disadvantages:

- Sometime extra overheads while passing data through layers.
- Sometimes takes long development time.
- More number of layers add complexities.
- Clean separation of each layer is difficult.
- Performance should be degraded due to multiple layers.

Application:

- When there is a need of multilevel security.
- Used when building new facilities on top of existing systems.

Client-Server architecture:

- It is one of the basic paradigms of distributing computing system.
- Main two components: clients and servers.
- A constraint of this style is – a client can communicate with the server and can't communicate with other clients.
- The communication between these components is initiated by the client when client sends a request for some services to the server and server responds them.
- The server receives the request at its predefined port, performs the service and then returns the results to the particular client.
- In it, request/reply type is working as a connector type.

Advantages:

- We can use the functionality of the server throughout the network.
- Provide centralized control.
- Data and file back up become easier.

Disadvantages:

- Performance may be unpredictable.
- Should have problem of overload and congestion.
- More expensive to install and manage.
- Skilled staffs are required for better maintenance.

Application:

- applicable when data in a shared database has to be accessed from different locations

Repository architecture: (Shared data)

- It in, all the data in a system is managed in a central repository.
- There are two types of components à data repositories and data assessors.
- Large amount of data sharing is possible.
- Different components do not need to communicate each other and not even need to know each other's' presence.
- In this style of architecture, read/write data to the repository works as connectors.
- Example à MIS

Pipe and filter architecture:

- It provides a structure for systems that process a stream of data.
- Data are passed through pipes between adjacent filters.
- In this architecture, filters are working components and pipes are working as connectors.
- Filter has interfaces from which a set of inputs can flow in and a set of outputs can flow out.
- Filters are independent entities, and they don't know the identity of other filters.
- The pipes are the connectors between a data source and the first filter, between filters, and between the last filter and a data sink.

Advantages:

- It is easy to understand and implement.
- Maintenance is easy and provides reusability.
- Filters can work parallel in multi-processing environment, so concurrent execution is also possible.
- This work flow style is used in many business processes.

Disadvantages:

- As filters are independent entities, designer has to provide complete transformation of input and output to each filter.
- This type of architecture not really suitable for interactive systems.
- Error handling is difficult in this type of architecture.

Application: Well suited for batch operating system.

Application Architecture

- Software application architecture is the process of defining a structured solution that meets all of the technical and operational requirements.
- Application architecture is the organizational design of an entire software application, including all sub-components and external applications.
- Application architecture helps us to understand the operations of the system.
- It describes the layout of application's deployment.
- It can be used as a blueprint to ensure that the underlying modules of an application will support future growth of the system.

Use of application architecture:

- It can be used as a starting point for architectural design.
- It is used as a design check list.
- It is used as a way of organizing the work of the development team.
- Different application architectures:
    - *Data processing application*
    - *Transaction processing application*
    - *Event processing system*
    - *Language processing system*

Data processing application

- It is data driven application that processes data in batches without explicit user interference during the processing.
- In it, data is input and output in batches.
- For example, in electricity billing system.
- This type of application usually has an à input-processing-output structure.
- Example à DFD.

Transaction Processing System (TPS)

- This is a data centered application.
- Transaction processing is a way of computing that divides work into individual, indivisible operations, called transactions. A **transaction processing system** (**TPS**) is a software system
- Users make asynchronous requests for service which are then processed by a transaction manager.
- Query processing takes place in the system database, and results are sent back to database through transaction manager.
- For example a reservation system.

Event Processing System.

- In which, system's actions are depend on events of system's environment.
- This system responds to events in the system environment.
- Due to unpredictable timing of events, architecture has to be organized to handle this.
- For example word processing system and real time systems.

Language processing system.

- In which, accept a natural or artificial language as input and generate some other representation of that language.
- It includes the translator or interpreter to generate the output language.
- Best example for this system is compiler which translates high level programming language into lower level (machine code).

III

Software Project Management

Responsibilities of software project manager

- Responsibilities of software project manager
- Responsible for accomplishing the stated project objectives.
- Take the overall responsibility of project success.
- The job responsibility is Planning to Deployment
- Bridging gap between the production team and client.
- Manage project management triangle which are Cost, Time, Scope and Quality.
- General activities: like project proposal writing, project cost estimation, scheduling, project staffing, software process tailoring, project monitoring and control, software configuration management, risk management, interfacing with clients, managerial report writing and presentations, etc.
- Mainly à project planning and controlling.
- Risk management.
- Time and cost estimation.

Skills of project manager

- Must have theoretical knowledge.
- A good decision-making capability.
- He should be client representative.
- Should have management skill.
- Focuses on risk management.
- He should have team leadership skill.
- He should have the experience in the related area.
- Monitoring and scheduling capability.

Metrics for project size estimation

- Metrics are the tools that help in better monitoring and control.
- Size of the program (or project) is neither the number of bytes that the source code occupies nor the byte size of the executable code.
- But it is an indicator of the **effort and time** required to develop the project. So, it indicates project development complexity.
- **The project size is a measure of the problem complexity** in terms of the effort and time required to develop the product.
- There are several metrics to measure problem size. Each of them has its own advantages and disadvantages.
- Two important metrics to estimate size:
    - Lines of code (LOC)
    - Function point.
    - Lines of Code (LOC)

- Simplest measure, Very popular due to simplicity.
- The project size is estimated by **counting the number of source instructions** in the developed program. (No commonest line)
- To estimate LOC à project manager divides the problem into modules and sub modules, until leaf level modules can be estimated.

Function point metric (FP)

- FP is directly dependent on the number of different functions or features it supports.
- This metric overcomes many of the shortcomings of the LOC metric.
- Function point metrics, **measure functionality from the users' point of view.**
- One of the important advantages of using the function point metric is that it can be used to easily estimate the size of a software product **directly from the problem specification.**
- **FP considers five different characteristics of the product** to calculate the size. The function point (FP) of given software is the weighted sum of these five items, and it will give unadjusted function point (UFP).

"UFP = (Number of inputs)*4 +(Number of outputs)*5 +(Number of inquiries)*4 +(Number of files)*10 +(Number of interfaces)*10"

- Once the **unadjusted function point (UFP)** is computed, **the technical complexity factor (TCF) is computed next.**
- **TCF refines the UFP by considering 14 factors** which assigns 0 (no influence) to 6 (strong influence). These numbers are summed and yielding DI (Degree of Influence).
- Now TCF is computed as **TCF = (0.65 + 0.01 * DI)**
- As DI can vary from 0 to 70, TCF can vary from 0.65 to 1.35.
- **Finally: FP = UFP * TCF**

Scheduling

Types Of Scheduling

1. Work breakdown structure (WBS)
2. Activity network and Critical Path Method (CPM)
3. GANTT Chart
4. Project monitoring and control

Work breakdown Structure (WBS)

- WBS is used to **decompose a given task** set recursively into small activities.
- The WBS is a uniform, consistent, and logical method for dividing the project into small, manageable components for purposes of **planning, estimating, and monitoring.**
- **Provides systematic planning**, key project elements and simplifies the project by dividing into small manageable units.
- **Provide roadmap for** à resource allocation, scheduling, budgeting, productivity, performance etc.
- WBS can be **graphically shown in a hierarchical tree structure.**
- In which, root node is labeled by a problem name. Each node of the tree is broken down into smaller activities that are made the children of the node.
- WBS can be done by the **decision of the project manager.**

Types of WBS

- **Process WBS: decomposes large processes into smaller ones.**
- **Product WBS:decomposes large entities into smaller ones.**
- **Hybrid WBS:in includes both process and product elements into single WBS.**

- There are two methods of WBS presentation:
- Tree structure
- Indented list form

Activity Network

- Activities in a project are graphically represented using activity network diagram.
- Activity network is a network graph using nodes with interconnecting edges to represent tasks and their planned sequence of completion, interdependence and interrelationship that must be accomplished to reach the project goals.
- It finds out the most efficient sequence of events needed to complete a project.

Activity diagram graphically showing:

- **The total amount of time** needed to complete the project
- **The sequence** in which tasks must be carried out
- Which tasks can be carried out at the same time
- Which are the **critical tasks** that you need to keep an eye on.

Critical Path Method (CPM)

- Critical path is the **sequence of activities with the longest duration and critical activities.**
- CPM used to **calculate project completion time.**
- **The project manager** identifies the critical path for the project.
- CPM deals with **both cost and time.**
- It is based on **single time estimation.**

Need of CPM

- Planning resource requirements.
- Control resource allocation.
- Prediction of deliverables.
- Internal and external program review.
- Performance evaluation.

Advantages of CPM

- It provides clear, concise and unambiguous way of documenting project plans, schedules, time and cost.
- It is mathematically easy and simple.
- It is useful to new project managers.
- It displays dependencies which help in scheduling.
- It determines slack time.
- It can display parallel running activity.
- It is widely used in industry purpose.

Disadvantages of CPM

- **Too complex** for large projects.

- It doesn't handle the scheduling of people and resource allocation.
- Critical path should be **calculated carefully**.
- Calculation of estimating the completion time is difficult.
- Activity **time estimates are subjective** and depend on judgment.

GANTT Chart

- It was proposed by Henry Gantt in 1914, also called **time line chart.**
- It is mainly **used to allocate resources to activities** (Resource Planning).
- The resources allocated to activities include staff, hardware, and software etc.
- A Gantt chart is a special type of bar chart where each bar represents an activity. Bars are drawn along time line. Length of bar proportional to the duration of time planned.
- It shows **activities against time**.
- **Slack time** is also shown in the bars.
- The chart is **prepared by the project manager**.

How to plan GANTT chart:

- Identify all the tasks.
- If possible, break down the tasks into smaller tasks.
- Determine the total estimated completion time for each task.
- Plot activities on GANTT chart. Draw milestones at applicable places.

Advantages

- Simple to understand and easy to use.
- Useful for planning and guiding projects, understating critical paths & planning resources.
- It is used in monitoring the progress of the project.

Disadvantages

- It doesn't show interdependencies and precedence of activities.
- Not suitable for large projects.

- It can't calculate shortest time for any activity in the project.

GANTT chart example:

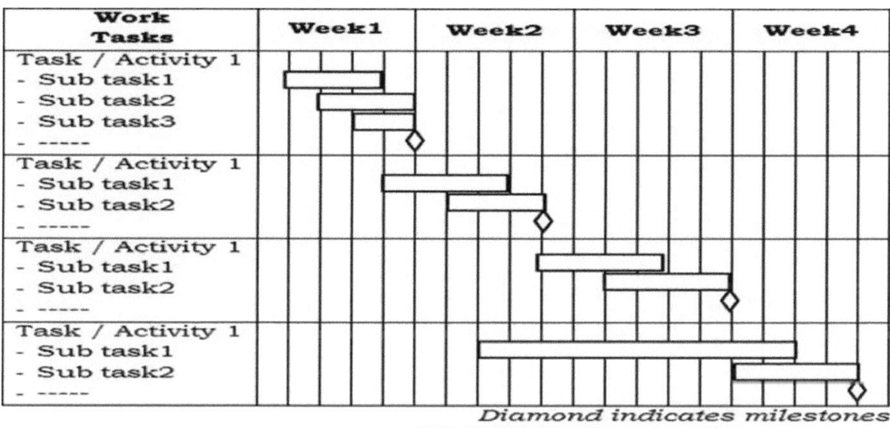

GANTT chart example.

Project Monitoring and Control

- Planning is one of the most important activities of project.
- ***Monitoring*** – collecting, recording, and reporting information
- ***Controlling*** – uses data from monitor activity to bring actual performance from planned performance.
- ***Project monitoring and planning (PMC)***activities take place in parallel with project execution, so the implementation should be corrective at appropriate level.
- The main purpose is to make sure that the project plan is being followed and also forecast future performance.

Need of PMC

- To detect and react appropriately to deviations and changes to plans.
- ***We need to monitor*** à men, machine, money, material, space, time, tasks, quality, performance and ***we need to control*** à time, cost and performance.

PMC activities:

- Comparing the work.
- Assessing work performance.
- Analyzing, tracking, monitoring, and reporting on project risks.
- Providing reports.
- Monitoring the implementation of approved changes.
- Do scope verification, quality and cost control.
- Ensuring of defect repairs.
- Take correct actions when needed.

Risk Management

- **Software risk** is a problem that could cause some loss or threaten the success of software project, but which hasn't happened yet.
- This risk may **affect negatively** to the cost, schedule, technical success or quality of the project.
- **Risk management** is the process of identifying, addressing and eliminating these problems before they can damage the project.
- **Objectives of the risk management**
- **Identify potential problems** and deal with them when they are easier to handle before they become critical.
- **Focus on the project's objectives** and consciously look after.
- **Allow early identification of risks** and provide management.
- Increase the chance of project success.

Risk management activities

Risk assessment

- It is the process of examining a project and identifying areas of potential risk.
- It includes the following activities:

- **Risk identification**
- **Risk analysis**
- **Risk prioritization**

Risk identification

- It is a systematic attempt to specify threats of the project plan.
- **Purpose** à to develop list of risk items also called *risk statement*
- Some common risks areas are found and checklist is prepared.
- *Categorize risks* into different classes.
- The project manager can then examine which risks from each class are relevant to the project.

- There are three main categories of risks:

I. **Project risks:** budgetary, schedule, personnel, resource etc.
II. **Technical risks:** Risks that threaten the quality of the product. design, implementation, interfacing, testing, and maintenance problems etc.

    ◦ Most technical risks occur due to improper knowledge.

I. **Business risks:** Risks that threaten the development (or client) organization. Include risks of building an excellent product that no one wants, losing budgetary or personnel commitments, etc.

Risk analysis

- When the risks have been identified, all risks are analyzed using different criteria.
- **The purpose** of this activity is à to examine how project outcomes might change with modification of risk input variables.
- **The input** of this activity is à the list of risks developed in risk identification and **output is** à the ranking of the risks.

▪ **Risk Prioritization**

- It **focuses on its most severe risks** by assessing the risk.
- Risks are **estimated in probability** of (0.1 – 1.0).
- The higher the exposure, the more the risk should be tackled.
- Another way is à **risk avoidance** (don't do risky things).

Risk Control

- It is the process of managing risks to achieve the desired outcomes.
- It includes:

1. Risk management planning
2. Risk monitoring
3. Risk resolution

Risk management planning

- Provides plan to deal with risk.
- Identify different strategies, like:
    - Risk avoidance (don't do risky things)
    - Risk minimization [risk reduction] (reduce impact of risks)
    - Risk contingency plan (deals with risks if it occurs)

Risk resolution

- Risk resolution is the execution of the plans for dealing with each risk.
- Decided by project manager.
- The input of this activity is à risk action plan
- And out puts area

- Risk status - Acceptable risks - Reduced rework
- Corrective actions - Problem prevention

Project Estimation Techniques

- Project estimation can estimate project size, cost, duration and required effort.
- There are three categories of estimation techniques:
    - Empirical estimation technique
    - Heuristic technique
    - Analytical estimation technique

Empirical estimation technique

- Empirical estimation techniques are based on making an educational guess of project parameters.
- Depends on the prior experience and domain knowledge of the project.
- There are two most popular empirical techniques:

a. Expert judgment
q. Delphi estimation technique

Expert judgment

- In this technique, an expert makes an educated guess of the problem size after analyzing the problem thoroughly.
- Usually, the expert estimates the cost of the different components that would make up the system and then combines the estimates for the individual modules to arrive at the overall estimate.
- However, this technique is subject to human errors and individual bias.
- It may possible that every time expert may not have experience and good knowledge of all the features of project.
- For ex. He may be aware of database and user interface parts but may not aware of coding part.
- A more refined form of expert judgment is the estimation made by a group of experts.

Delphi estimation technique

- Delphi cost estimation technique tries to overcome some of the shortcomings of the expert judgment approach.
- Delphi estimation is carried out by a team comprising of a group of experts and a coordinator.
- In this approach, the coordinator provides each estimator with a copy of the software requirement specification (SRS) document and a form for recording his cost estimate.
- Individual expert estimates secretly and submit them to coordinator.
- Coordinator then summarizes the response of all expert estimators.
- Prepared summary report is distributed to all estimators and based on this report expert estimators re-estimate the project.

Heuristic Technique

- Estimation in these techniques is performed with the help of mathematical equations.

Analytical Estimation Technique

- Unlike empirical and heuristic, in this estimation technique have certain scientific basis.
- Halstead's software science is an example of an analytical technique.
- Halstead's software science is especially useful for estimating software maintenance.

IV

Software Coding and Testing

INTRODUCTION – CODING

- The objective of coding phase is to transform the design of a system into code in a high-level language.

CODE REVIEW

- Code review for a model is carried out after all the syntax errors have been eliminated.
- This is the cost-effective strategies for reduction in coding errors and to produce high quality code.
- Two types code review techniques are **code inspection** and **code walk through**.

Code walk through

- Code walk through is a **code analysis technique**.
- In this technique carried out after a module has been coded, successfully compiled and all syntax errors eliminated.
- A few members of the development team are given the code few days before the walk through meeting to read and understand code.

- The main objectives of the walk through are to find the algorithmic and logical errors in the code.
- The members note down their findings to discuss these in a walk through meeting
- Some of the guidelines for this technique:

  - It should consist of between three to seven members.
  - Discussion should focus on find the errors and not on how to fix the errors.
  - Managers should not attend the walk through meetings.

Code Inspection

- The aim of code inspection is to discover common types of errors caused due to improper programming.
- During code inspection the code is examined for the presence of certain kinds of errors.
- Error will be discovered by looking for these kinds of mistakes in the code.
- Coding standards is also checked during code inspection.
- Good software development companies collect different types of errors commonly committed by their engineers and identify the type of errors most frequently committed.
- List of commonly committed errors can be used during code inspection to look out for possible errors.
- Following is a list of some errors which can be checked during code inspection:

  - Use of uninitialized variables
  - No terminating loops
  - Incompatible assignments
  - Improper storage allocation and deallocation
  - Mismatches between actual and formal parameter in procedure calls
  - Use of incorrect logical operators or incorrect precedence among operators

Software Documentation

- When a software product is developed, in addition to the executable files and the source code, several kinds of documents such as users' manual, SRS document, design document, test document, installation manual etc. are developed as part of the software engineering process.
- **Good documents are very useful and serve the following purposes.**
    - Good documents help enhance understandability of software product.
    - Documents help the users to understand an effectively use the system.

Different types of software documents can be classified into the following:

- **Internal Documentation:**
    - These are provided in the source code itself.
- **External Documentation:**
    - These are the supporting documents that usually accompany a software product.

Internal documentation

- Documentation which focuses on the information that is used to determine the software code is known as internal documentation.
- It describes the data structures, algorithms, and control flow in the programs.
- The important types of internal documentation are the following:
    - Comments embedded in the source code
    - Use of meaningful variable names
    - Module and function headers
    - Code structuring

External Documentation

- Documentation which focuses on **general description** of the software code is known as external documentation.
- It includes information such as function of code, name of the software developer who has written the code, format of the output produced by the software.
- It consists of information such as description of the problem along with the program written to solve it.
- For the purpose of readability and proper understanding, the detailed description is given by figures and illustrations that how one component is related to another.

Testing

- The **basic goal** of any software development is to produce software that has no errors or has few errors.
- Testing is relied on **to detect the faults**. Testing is itself an expensive activity.
- If **program fails to behave as expected**, it needs to be debugged and corrected. For that testing is done.
- **Testing is the process of executing a program to locate an error.**
- In testing, program is provided a set of test inputs (test cases).
- **Aim of testing** à to identify all defects existing in a software product.

Some commonly used terms associated with testing are:

- Error: a kind of mistake (syntax or logical error).
- Bug: mistake done by programmer at the time of coding.
- Fault: it is representation of an error.
- Failure: occurs when fault executes, it is demonstration of an error.
- Test case: it is a Triplet [I,S,O].
- Test suit: set of all test cases.

Black box testing

- This method is also called **behavioral testing or functional testing.**
- It is a technique of testing without having any knowledge of the internal working of the application.

- That is, test cases are designed based on an analysis of the input/output behavior and does not require any knowledge of the internal structure of a program.
- For this reason, black-box testing is also known as functional testing.
- Tester must know the system architecture.

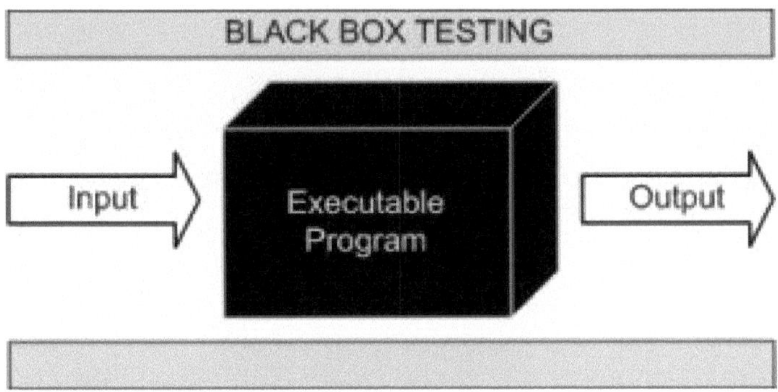

- This method attempts to find errors in the following categories:
  - Incorrect or missing functions
  - Interface errors
  - Errors in data structures or external database access
  - Behavior or performance errors
  - Initialization and termination errors

White box testing

- This method is concerned with **testing the implementation** of the program.
- **The aim** of this testing is to investigate the internal logic and structure of the code. That is why white box testing is also called **structural testing.**
- In white box testing it is necessary for a tester to have **full knowledge of source code.**
- In white-box approach, test cases are based on an analysis of the code.

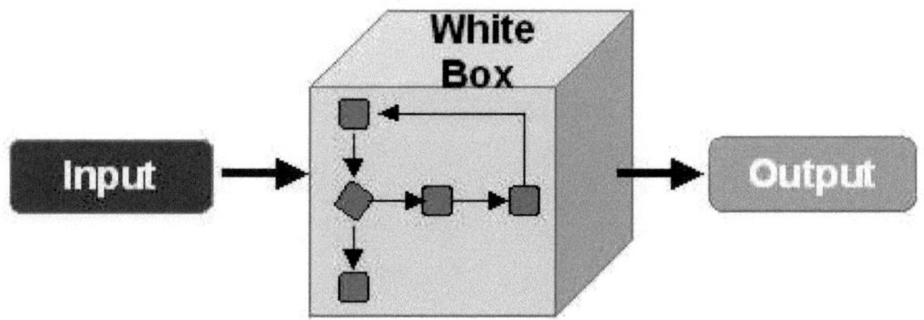

Test documentation

- The documentation which is generated towards the end of testing is the test summary reports.
- It provides summary of test suits which has been applied to the system.
- It specifies how many test suits are successful, how many are unsuccessful and what is the degree of successful and unsuccessful.

MULTIPLE CHOICE QUESTION

1. What are the characteristics of software?

A. Software is developed or engineered; it is not manufactured in the classical sense.
B. Software doesn't "wear out".
C. Software can be custom built or custom build.
D. All mentioned above

Answer: D. All mentioned above

2. Software is defined as ____.

A. Instructions
B. Data Structures
C. Documents
D. All of the above

Answer: D. All mentioned above

3. What are the signs that a software project is in trouble?

A. The product scope is poorly defined.
B. Deadlines are unrealistic.
C. Changes are managed poorly.
D. All of the above

Answer: D. All mentioned above

4. You are working as a project manager. Your Company wants to develop a project. You are also involved in planning team. What will be your first step in project planning?

A. Establish the objectives and scope of the product.
B. Requirement Gathering
C. Project Definition
D. Project Planning

Answer: A. Establish the objectives and scope of the product.

5. A Project can be characterized as _____ .

A. Every project may not have a unique and distinct goal.
B. Project is routine activity or day-to-day operations.
C. Project does not come with a start time and end time.
D. None of the above

Answer: D. None of the above

6. Identify the correct statement: "Software engineers shall

A. Act in a manner that is in the best interests of his expertise and favor.
B. Act consistently with the public interest
C. Ensure that their products only meet the SRS.
D. None of the above

Answer: B. Act consistently with the public interest

7. What is a Software?

A. Software is set of programs
B. Software is documentation and configuration of data
C. Both a and b
D. None of the mentioned

Answer: C. Both a and b

8. What are attributes of good software?

A. Software maintainability
B. Software functionality
C. Software development
D. Both A and B

Answer: D. Both A and B

9. Which of these software engineering activities are not a part of software processes?

A. Software dependence
B. Software development
C. Software validation

D. Software specification

Answer: A. Software dependence

10.Which of the following activities of a Generic Process framework provides a feedback report?

A. Communication
B. Planning
C. Modeling & Construction
D. Deployment

Answer: D. Deployment

11.Which one of the following is not a fundamental activity for software processes in software engineering?

A. Software Verification
B. Software Validation
C. Software design and implementation
D. Software evolution

Answer: A. Software Verification

12.Which of the following is/are considered stakeholder in the software process?

A. Customers
B. End-users
C. Project managers
D. All of the above

Answer: D. All of the above

13.What is the main aim of Software engineering?

A. Reliable software
B. Cost effective software
C. Reliable and cost-effective software
D. None of the above

Answer: C. Reliable and cost-effective software

14.RAD Software process model stands for _____.

A. Rapid Application Development
B. Relative Application Development.
C. Rapid Application Design.
D. Recent Application Development.

Answer: A. Rapid Application Development

15.What is the simplest model of software development paradigm?

A. Spiral model
B. Big Bang model
C. V-model
D. Waterfall model

Answer: D. Waterfall model

16.Which one of the following is not a phase of Prototyping Model.

A. Quick Design
B. Coding
C. Prototype Refinement
D. Engineer Product

Answer: B. Coding

17.RAD Model has?

A. 2 phases
B. 3 phases
C. 5 phases
D. 6 phases

Answer: C. 5 phases

18. SDLC stands for

A. Software Development Life Cycle
B. System Development Life cycle
C. Software Design Life Cycle
D. System Design Life Cycle

Answer: A. Software Development Life Cycle

20. Which model can be selected if user is involved in all the phases of SDLC?

A. Waterfall Model
B. Prototyping Model
C. RAD Model
D. both b & c

Answer: C. RAD Model

21.Identify the disadvantage of Spiral Model.

A. Doesn't work well for smaller projects
B. High amount of risk analysis
C. Strong approval and documentation control
D. Additional Functionality can be added

Answer: A. Doesn't work well for smaller projects

22.Find out which phase is not available in SDLC?

A. Coding
B. Testing
C. Maintenance
D. Abstraction

Answer: D. Abstraction

23.Which of the items listed below is not one of the software engineering layers?

A. Process
B. Manufacturing
C. Methods
D. Tools

Answer: B. Manufacturing

24. Design phase is followed by ______.

A. Coding

B. Testing
C. Maintenance
D. None of the above.

Answer: A. Coding

25.The advantages of creating a prototype are

A. It can serve as means of communication between developers and customers
B. It allows developers to experiment with number of different design options
C. Both (a) and (b)
D. None of the above

Answer: C. Both (a) and (b)

26. Where is the prototyping model of software development well suited?

A. When requirements are well defined.
B. For projects with large development teams.
C. When a customer cannot define requirements clearly
D. None of the above.

Answer: C. When a customer cannot define requirements clearly

27. What is the meaning of requirement elicitation in software engineering?

A. Gathering of requirement.
B. Understanding of requirement.
C. Getting the requirements from client.
D. All of the above

Answer: D. All of the above

28. If requirements are easily understandable and defined then which model is best suited?

A. Spiral model
B. Waterfall model

C. Prototyping model
D. None of the above

Answer: B. Waterfall model

29. Software consists of ______.

A. Set of instructions + operating procedures
B. Programs + documentation
C. Programs + hardware manuals
D. Set of programs

Answer: B. Programs + documentation

30. The process of developing a software product using software engineering principles and methods is referred to as, _______.

A. Software myths
B. Scientific Product
C. Software Evolution
D. None of the above

Answer: C. Software Evolution

1. Spiral model is a combination of both Iterative model and one of the SDLC model.

A. True
B. False

Answer: A. True

32. What is the main aim of Software engineering?

A. Reliable software
B. Cost effective software
C. Reliable and cost-effective software
D. None of the above

Answer: C. Reliable and cost-effective software

33. Which is the most important feature of spiral model?

A. Quality management
B. Risk management
C. Performance management
D. Efficiency management

Answer: B. Risk management

34. ER model shows the _______ .

A. Static view
B. Functional view
C. Dynamic view
D. All the above

Answer: B. Functional view

35. A good design review is not important for good software design and its accuracy and quality.

A. True
B. False

Answer: B. False

36. Every attribute is defined by its corresponding set of values, called Attributes.

A. True
B. False

Answer: B. False

37. Every attribute is defined by its corresponding set of values is called ______.

A. Entity

B. Domain
C. Relationship
D. None of the above

Answer: B. Domain

38. Which type of DFD concentrates on the system process and flow of data in the system?

A. Logical DFD
B. Physical DFD
C. Both A & B
D. None of the above

Answer: A. Logical DFD

39. Which coupling is also known as "Global coupling"?

A. Content coupling
B. Stamp coupling
C. Data coupling
D. Common coupling

Answer: D. Common coupling

40. Modularization is a technique to divide a software system into multiple discrete and independent modules.

A. True
B. False

Answer: A. True

41. An entity in ER Model is a real world being, which has some properties called_____.

A. Attributes
B. Relationship

C. Domain
D. None of the above

Answer: A. Attributes

42. _____ is measure of the degree of intercedence between modules.

A. Cohesion
B. Coupling
C. Modulus
D. None of the above

Answer: B. Coupling

43. In what type of coupling, the complete data structure is passed from one module to another?

A. Control Coupling
B. Stamp Coupling
C. External Coupling
D. Content Coupling

Answer: B. Stamp Coupling

44. _____ uses powerful development software and small ,highly trained teams of programmers.

A. Prototyping
B. RAD
C. Coding
D. Modeling

Answer: B. RAD

45. Which of the following is true about E-R Diagrams?

A. They consist of Object relationship pairs
B. It indicates cardinality of relationships

C. It indicates modality of relationships
D. all of the above

Answer: D. all of the above

46. which of the following is graphical tool for software design?

A. Data Flow Diagram
B. Structure Chart
C. Decision Tree
D. all of the above

B. Answer: D. all of the above

47. The most important feature of spiral model is

A. requirement gathering
B. risk management
C. quality management
D. configure management

Answer: B. risk management

48. The worst type of coupling is?

A. Data Coupling
B. Control Coupling
C. Stamp Coupling
D. Content Coupling

Answer: D. Content Coupling

49. which phase is not available in software life cycle?

A. Coding
B. Testing
C. Maintenance
D. Abstraction

Answer: D. Abstraction

50. Which is not step of requirement engineering?

    A. Requirement Gathering
    B. Requirement Analysis
    C. Requirement Design
    D. Requirement Documentation

Answer: C. Requirement Design

51. Effective software project management focuses on four P's which are

A. people, performance, payoff, product
B. people, product, performance, process
C. people, product, process, project
D. People, process, Payoff, Product

Answer: C. people, product, process, project

52. A project is considered successful when:

A. The product of the project has been manufactured.
B. The project sponsor announces the completion of the project.
C. The product of the project is turned over to the operations area to handle the ongoing aspects of the project.
D. The project meets or exceeds the expectations of the stakeholders.

Answer: D. The project meets or exceeds the expectations of the stakeholders.

53. What are the triple constraints?

A. Time, schedules, and quality
B. Time, availability, and quality
C. Time, money, and schedules
D. Time, money, and quality

Answer: D. Time, money, and quality

54. Projects have predetermined

A. Time Span
B. Budget
C. none of them
D. Both A and B

Answer: D. Both A and B

55. The process each manager follows during the life of a project is known as

A. Project Management
B. Manager life cycle
C. Project Management Life Cycle
D. All of the mentioned

Answer: C. Project Management Life Cycle

56. Which of the following term describes testing?

A. Finding broken code
B. Evaluating deliverable to find errors
C. A stage of all projects
D. None of the mentioned

Answer: B. Evaluating deliverable to find errors

57. White Box techniques are also classified as

A. Design based testing
B. Structural testing
C. Error guessing technique
D. None of the mentioned

Answer: B. Structural testing

58. What are the various Testing Levels?

A. Unit Testing
B. System Testing
C. Integration Testing
D. All of the mentioned

Answer: D. All of the mentioned

59. Test cases are designed during:

A. Test recording.
B. Test configuration.
C. Test planning.
D. Test specification

Answer: D. Test specification

60. What do you understand by V&V in software testing?

A. Verified Version

B. Version Validation

C. Verification and Validation

D. Version Verification

Answer: C. Verification and Validation

Printed by Libri Plureos GmbH in Hamburg,
Germany